OF01032

Books should be returned to the SDH Library on or before
the date stamped above unless a renewal has been arranged

Salisbury District Hospital Library

Telephone: Salisbury (01722) 336262 extn. 4430 / 33
Out of hours answer machine in operation

Other titles in the Palliative Care series include:

Why is it so difficult to die? by Brian Nyatanga
Hidden Aspects of Palliative Care by Brian Nyatanga and
Maxine Astley-Pepper
Fundamental Aspects of Palliative Care Nursing by Robert Becker and
Richard Gamlin

series editor: Brian Nyatanga

Counselling Skills in Palliative Care

Jean Bayliss

Quay Books
MA Healthcare Limited

Quay Books Division, MA Healthcare Limited, Jesses Farm, Snow Hill, Dinton,
Salisbury, Wiltshire, SP3 5HN

British Library Cataloguing-in-Publication Data
A catalogue record is available for this book

© MA Healthcare Limited 2004
ISBN 1 85642 234 8

Printed in the UK by Cromwell Press, Trowbridge, Wiltshire

To Derek

Contents

Foreword

The complex psychological and emotional needs encountered by professional healthcare workers while caring for those with life-threatening illness, are varied and demanding. Palliative care, involving terminally ill patients and their relatives, poses one of the biggest challenges to healthcare professionals to ensure that care is individually tailored, sensitive and effective. There is a real need for all healthcare professionals to develop an in-depth understanding of loss in the broadest sense and this includes multiple and cumulative losses. This should be followed by a specific appreciation of loss in relation to dying and following death. Such understanding and appreciation should be accompanied by a development of helping or counselling 'helping' skills necessary to support the patient and family. There is a fine line between helping others to come to terms with their loss and finding yourself as the carer being supported by the bereaved. Without the appropriate level of skill it may be possible that a dying patient, and later the bereaved, may end up supporting the carer if too much personal disclosure happens. The development of counselling 'helping' skills is important to every healthcare professional who cares for the dying patient and his or her family unit.

In this book, Jean Bayliss has acknowledged both the complexity of the needs and the role of helping skills required for professionals in providing such important and supportive care. The book explores the issues of loss in general and specific to dying. The complex concepts encountered in death and dying have been explained clearly and simply to help both novices and experienced professionals in their caring roles. It is encouraging to see how complex theories and models on loss and bereavement respectively have been systematically 'unpacked' to allow greater understanding by the reader. Such skill should be applauded, as most books in the past have tended to be jargonistic, and less meaningful to the reader. The style of this book enables the reader to work through some questions during each chapter, and a summary at the end helps to capture the key points in that chapter. This allows time and space to reflect on some of the discussion points in each chapter. Readers will be encouraged to develop their critical analysis skills as they work through the text. The book will be valuable for those in search of basic (essential) counselling skills and those yearning for advanced skills. Both professionals and informal carers will find some informative chapters to help their own understanding of loss and its impact.

Counselling Skills in Palliative Care is a welcome addition to educators and trainers facilitating communication and counselling skills. The scenarios and work-through type questions found in the book will be useful for educators in their preparation for and presentation of teaching sessions. The text can be a useful companion for educators running communication and counselling skills courses up to degree level. University and hospice libraries will find this book a welcome addition to their shelves.

I personally feel that Jean has provided a book that will help reduce the fear and desperation that most 'helpers' often find themselves in while trying to support dying patients and their relatives. I would like to congratulate Jean on this comprehensive and timely text on such a sensitive topic.

Finally, while Jean was writing this book, her husband Derek, also a dear friend, became seriously ill and died peacefully at their home in Worcestershire. The memory of Derek should be captured and remembered through this book; he was genuinely inspirational to Jean, myself and all those who knew him. It is only fitting that this book should be dedicated to Derek Bayliss.

Brian Nyatanga
Macmillan Senior Lecturer
April, 2004

Introduction

It is a paradox that there can be few, if any, times when we are more vulnerable than when we ourselves or those for whom we care are involved in the terminal phases of living; yet close contact with mortality seems to pose a threat, and this affects meaningful communication just when it is most needed. Perhaps the threat lies in the questions posed for all of us when we come close to mortality. Patients (the very word can sometimes rob us of individuality) in the final stages of their living-dying journey can be hurt in many ways, as they struggle not only with their own needs and wants, but with the needs and wants of their carers, both informal and professional. Palliative care can be a time when professionals learn a great deal about themselves, especially about their own fears, and many find it difficult to sustain a sense of personal effectiveness in the face of the great mystery that confronts them. Informal carers, friends and relatives may similarly learn much about themselves, about the dynamic of their relationship with the dying person and about their own attitudes to mortality. How to make this a time of positive learning, especially by offering insights into effective communication, is the chief aim of this book.

I have cared for my husband through to his death and the observations and insights offered here come from a personal as well as from a more academic perspective. My experience convinced me that attitudes to dying people is the crucial factor in the ability to relate to them and to those closest to them. It is attitudes which determine the quality of communication, which in turn is a crucial factor if palliative care is to be truly holistic. The paradox posed by the imminence of death sadly seems too often to inhibit meaningful communication just when everyone involved desperately wants to fulfil the wishes and needs of the dying person and those closest to him or her.

This book is an attempt to help with communication in palliative care — an area that is potentially stressful for the dying person, those closest to him or her, and for professionals. As a counsellor/therapist, it is perhaps inevitable that I should see the counselling approach to communication as the optimum way. This approach enables carers to grow more aware of their own feelings and opens up options for communicating via the use of counselling skills. The counselling approach is more than a set of skills, valuable though these are; it is underpinned by a set of values and qualities.

The carer who can develop the qualities — especially those of empathy, genuineness and acceptance — will find that expressing them through counselling skills will deepen and enrich interactions with the dying person. Thus, although the book describes and invites readers to practise counselling skills, it is as much concerned with relationship building and with developing the user of the skills in order to promote holistic care.

The journey through dying, to death and beyond to bereavement can be, and too often is, a lonely road. Offering companionship along that road is a gift, and this book aims to make that gift more meaningful by enhancing communication through counselling skills.

Jean Bayliss
April, 2004

1

What is loss?

All readers of this book have at least two things in common:

> We are all mortal;
> We have all experienced some form of loss.

The first commonality may be something which we choose not to think about too often, or — especially if we work in the field of palliative care — we may have a heightened awareness of our own vulnerability. (We look at this in greater detail in later chapters.) The second commonality — that we have all experienced some form of loss — is more variable than the absolute of death: the loss may vary from the trivial to the devastating. Even so, change and loss are part of the pattern of human existence. When people have a need for palliative care they, and those who love and are close to them, will have suffered many losses. If we are to help and support them, we need to understand the complexity of loss and to become as aware as possible of the meaning of these losses for the individuals concerned.

> Think of a time when a major change occurred in your life – it may have been a change that you chose and which brought about great benefit (especially in retrospect). Or, the change may have been imposed upon you by external influences or events. Make a list of the losses brought about by the change.

A major change in my own life was a move from employment, to self-employed consultancy. This was a long planned for and much wanted change, but it involved many losses:

- the certainty of a regular monthly salary
- the daily structure of getting myself to work and returning at more-or-less the same time each evening
- people; especially people to 'bounce ideas off'
- the ability to moan about 'them' as the cause of all problems

- the responsibility of having work given to me or allocated, and the ability to delegate
- the security of familiarity, both with setting and people, and my status with these.

Look again at your personal list of losses and at mine. Two aspects which seem to recur in loss are:

- the necessity to adapt to change
- the sense of missing someone or something.

> Try to look at the following major changes both in terms of the losses involved, and in the sense of missing something or someone and in terms of the need to adapt:
>
> 1. Moving to a much pleasanter house or locality
> 2. Moving into residential care
> 3. The arrival of a planned and longed for baby
> 4. A miscarriage
> 5. Theft of a car or bicycle
> 6. Promotion
>
> *Losses*   *Missing*   *Adapting*

Three of the best known theorists on loss who have given us some important guidelines for understanding these two aspects of adapting to change, and of 'missing' are: Peter Marris, John Bowlby and Colin Murray-Parkes.

In his book *Loss and Change* (1974), Marris offers us the interesting concept of structures of meaning. He suggests that we make sense of the world in which we live by creating patterns of familiarity. From birth onwards we attach meaning to people and objects. A baby in its cot or pram, for example, begins to attach meaning to the large shapes which loom over it — the meaning it attaches will be that such shapes mean food, comfort, survival (or, sadly, the reverse).

> Look at the following words and try to define what 'structure of meaning' each has for you:
>
> mother/father   home
> mealtimes   books
> holidays

The 'structure of meaning' around the word home may vary from security, place of refuge, to millstone because of the mortgage, endless rows, (and anything in between). It is unlikely that it will only mean, 16 The Avenue. These 'structures of meaning' tend to be carried with us through life from one situation to another: a child whose structures of meaning are that others in the world are well-meaning and positive, will react very differently in new situations from one whose structure of meaning is negative.

How often do you say, or hear others say, 'It means a lot to me'? Marris suggests that structures of meaning are so firmly embedded that they even appear in the language in this way. What 'means a lot' may vary from the first cup of tea of the day, to family, or to something like fairness or honesty, but all help us to make sense of our lives, at various levels. When loss occurs, it brings with it change in our 'structure of meaning' and adapting to this can be very painful, because it involves adapting not only to external changes but, sometimes, to our whole belief system.

At the time of writing, the world is still shaken by the destruction of the World Trade Centre in New York (and by other terrorist activities). The 'structures of meaning' this act demonstrated are very powerful (and equally powerfully opposed). News commentators frequently use the term 'the world will never be the same again', which illustrates how loss causes, and sometimes enforces, adaptation.

Marris's second concept is based on his view that humans have an innate or built in resistance to change. We are surrounded by change which we hardly notice (night becomes day; seasons rotate; children mature) and this makes us value predictability. When predictability is lost or threatened we feel unsettled and try to sustain the *status quo*. Marris calls this need to predict, the 'conservative impulse'. We need to be able to predict in order to make sense of what is happening to us, and to plan and, of course, planning tends to give us a sense of control. Marris says:

> .... *without continuity we cannot interpret what events mean to us, nor explore new kinds of experience with confidence.*

It is interesting that this impulse to conserve the familiar is also reflected in the language, 'things aren't what they used to be'; 'it was better when...'. There is often a yearning for the past (which can sometimes sentimentalise the past), because it was understood and therefore safe. The tag may be that, 'Familiarity breeds contempt', but it may be a greater truism that familiarity is essential for psychological wellbeing. An experience of major change, and the loss that accompanies it, would clearly be at odds with the need to conserve.

OFSTED – the United Kingdom Government's appointed inspection system for schools – find that many teachers are disillusioned with education. Comments like, 'I came into teaching to teach Maths/French/English. I don't want all these Key Stages. I don't want to be a social worker' are often quoted. Their dissatisfaction seems to illustrate Marris's sense that we prefer things as they were. It also illustrates the distress that losing a 'structure of meaning' (here, the belief that education was better in the past) can cause.

Perhaps closer to the palliative care theme we might reflect on changes which seem to be taking place in the hospice movement. James and Field (1992) suggested that there was a move towards more orthodox medical care and even a loosening of original hospice ideals:

> *Having originated outside the health care establishment as a critic of standards and practices of terminal care within NHS hospitals and elsewhere, the hospice movement has now become part of the mainstream of healthcare...*
>
> *This entry into the 'mainstream' has not been without its costs and problems for the hospice movement.*

Keeping Marris's ideas of 'structures of meaning' and 'conservatism' in mind, what losses and changes for the hospice movement might this entry into mainstream health care bring?

Some suggestions about the hospice movement's perceived change towards becoming an example of good practice in terminal care and an influence on policy making have been:

⌘ The traditional emphasis for insistence on physical intervention will be too strong to resist.
⌘ The organisation and hierarchy of hospices will mirror those of the institutions they originally tried to alter.
⌘ The rules and routines of traditional NHS care will, inevitably, be adopted.
⌘ The holistic approach will be lost.

You may not agree with these points, but the fears expressed illustrate Marris's views that we like to conserve the familiar and that we resist changes to structures of meaning – in this case the powerful 'meaning' of what terminal care should be.

The NHS itself and education are two huge organisations, affecting virtually everyone in the UK, and both have undergone enormous changes. One piece of research found that the NHS is a 'stressed' organisation and that the stress is almost entirely caused by changes. A piece of educational research showed that unless the volume and pace of change was stopped, teachers would feel so out of control that the rate of retention (already poor) would accelerate.

> Try to talk to an NHS worker and a teacher to examine their experiences of change in the light of Marris's theory.

Marris brings these two concepts together to help understand grief. Grieving is the process of adapting to loss, by regaining control of the environment. If you have ever been in hospital, or caught up in events over which you had no control, remind yourself of how important familiarity felt and of what you lost by feeling out of control of your environment or of yourself.

The second loss theorist, whose work has had a profound effect on child rearing practices and on how children in hospital are treated in the UK, is John Bowlby (1969).

> What do you understand by the term 'bonding'? What examples of this behaviour can you think of?

Bowlby's influential work on loss is based on his **theory of attachment** – that we humans have an innate need to attach ourselves to someone (or something), partly because our very survival may depend on it.

Just as 'it means a lot to me' has entered our day-to-day language, so has, 'I am (or was) very attached to …'.

> Write a list of objects, places or people that you are, or were, attached to and refer to it as we explore Bowlby's theory further.

For Bowlby, attachment is linked to our need for security and safety. When loss of that attachment is threatened, or actually occurs, it causes distress, 'The greater the degree of attachment, the greater the degree of loss.' Look at your list of attachments. What were your feelings when the attachment was broken? Or, how would you feel if some of them were to be broken? Bowlby suggests that in order to preserve attachments, we have developed a range of attachment behaviours – babies soon learn that if they coo, gurgle and smile the attachment figure stays closer for longer! From his observations of children, Bowlby thought that when what he called an 'affectional bond' is broken or threatened, we experience three stages or phases of loss:

- protest
- despair
- detachment.

Bowlby (1972) illustrates this by describing the separation of a young child from its mother. In the protest phase it will cling, cry, be very angry and demanding, as if the separation can be prevented. The child may then become quieter (often articulated by childminders as 's/he's always all right once you've gone'), but Bowlby does not see this as compliance, but as despair and he says that close observation will show a gradual loss of hope – the child will give up searching and gradually stop looking up hopefully every time the door is opened.

Finally, when hope is gone, the child seems to disattach so that it can sometimes seem not even to recognise the mother when she reappears. Bowlby's theories have had a great deal of influence on how adult mourning is thought of, but before we explore that in a later chapter, look at your list of losses and reflect whether they resonate with Bowlby's theory.

Two arguments made against Bowlby's theory are that his observations are based on Western childrearing practices (and these in themselves have undergone radical change in the past fifty years). Feminists have disputed his view that attachment to the mother is essential to psychological health.

Bowlby (1982) developed his attachment and separation theory to what he called a 'control theory of attachment'. We develop goal-orientated behaviours to maintain attachment and to give us control over our environment.

> What similarities can you see here with Marris?
> What differences?

In the field of palliative care, what are the 'attachments' which a patient might have had broken by a terminal diagnosis? What further attachments may have to be broken?

Bowlby (1980) termed the reactions to loss as 'separation anxiety'.

> What separation anxiety might you expect to see in a patient needing palliative care?

Murray-Parkes (1986) has been the consultant psychiatrist at St Christopher's Hospice (often seen as the 'flag ship' of the hospice movement because of its pioneering work). His theory of **psychosocial transition** brings together the psychological and sociological experience of loss, and while his work is focused especially on bereavement, his theory can apply to loss in a more general sense. Before we look at the theory, let's explore the idea of **transition**. The word itself contains the idea that it is something we move or pass through and will, therefore, involve a degree of change.

Recall a major change in your life and try to list the order in which you adapted (willingly or unwillingly) to the change. What, in retrospect, was the process through which you negotiated that change?

There are several models of transition — some quite complex — but the following fairly basic example is not untypical. As you read it, reflect on whether your personal transition followed a similar pattern.

Model of transition

1. An event which begins a transition marks a boundary – at the time it may not appear that this was so, but in retrospect, it is clear that there was a 'before' and an 'after'. As the transition begins, we are suspended between the past and the future.
2. As change begins there is a sense of some things ending. What *was* is no longer possible, or at least no longer possible as it was. There is therefore a period of modification, as the 'before' involves terminating relationships, rôles or different ways of being. This can be a time of loss or separation.
3. Questioning and reevaluation of who we were and are takes place. As the changes of stage 2 happen, the past, and the change itself are reflected on and questions about them emerge. 'Why?' is perhaps the most powerful question, especially if the change is unwanted. Sometimes the questioning can be very profound and may lead to loss

of or strengthening of faith. There may be considerable anxiety about whether we can cope with the modifications which have to be made.

4. New ways of living and being are experimented with and this experimenting is strongly influenced by the questioning and evaluation that took place at stage 3 of the transition. The testing out of new patterns may be exciting and challenging, or it may be daunting and overwhelming.

5. Commitment to the new patterns begins to take place. This does not necessarily mean a happy acceptance of the new roles, relationships, tasks, but more an acknowledgement that this is the way that things have to be from now on.

6. The acknowledgement of stage 5 moves us towards the end of the transition and into the new life — which may be fulfilling or bleak and uncertain.

Think of a person newly given a terminal diagnosis. Would this model of a transition seem to be the path they might tread? Or might they not move beyond stage 3?

Murray-Parkes's theory (1986) incorporates an aspect of transition into what he calls our 'assumptive worlds'. His view is that we live in a world of assumptions which can vary on a spectrum from the mundane to the profound: if you break off from reading this chapter and go to make yourself a drink, you assume that water will come from the tap and that when you return, you chair will still be waiting for you. We have similar internal, psychological assumptions – that our children will outlive us, perhaps, or that those we love and we ourselves, are likely to stay safe. This is what makes up our 'assumptive world', which is both social and psychological. When something happens to upset the assumptions, whether it is a power cut when we planned to read or watch television, or whether it is an unexpected death (or other 'assumption' on the spectrum) we enter a time of adaptation and adjustment, a psychosocial transition, as we build a new assumptive world. This can be a very painful process.

A criticism made of the assumptive world theory is that it is too Westernised – those who live with famine, war or where natural disasters happen live with uncertainty rather than assumption. The 11 September 2001 events in New York may give us pause here.

Think again about a person given a terminal diagnosis, but this time the person is a child. What assumptive world might the child's parents have had?

> What sort of psychosocial transition would be involved for them?
> What losses might they experience?

Murray-Parkes suggests three factors which make some psychosocial transitions more difficult:

⌘ A major revision of assumptions about the world and our place in it is needed.
⌘ The effects of the change are lasting.
⌘ They are relatively speedy, allowing little time for preparation.

There are similarities between the theory of 'structures of meaning' and 'assumptive worlds'; both, for instance, indicate that we need to predict in order to understand the world we live in, and both share with Bowlby some sense of 'separation' anxiety'. All three theories remind us that loss, and the change which accompanies it, is a lifelong experience and although humans are, on the whole, adaptable and resilient at coping with change, some losses test that resilience to the limit. The losses for life-limited people and those who care for them may be very testing indeed.

Some of the losses which a life-limited person suffers were listed by some hospice workers (professional and volunteers). They were specifically asked not to give them a rank order, but as you read through the list, try to think which would in your view require most adaptability in terms of the theories we have looked at.

Losses for a dying person (as seen by others):

- body image
- choice
- status
- independence
- control: emotional and other
- dignity
- future
- faculties
- personality/self
- faith
- peace of mind
- interests/hobbies
- social life

- income
- expectations
- ability to give pleasure
- enjoyment (eg. of food)
- comfort
- aims
- privacy
- normality
- relationships
- sexual relationship (and function)
- honesty
- hope.

Would you want to add to this list from your own experience? When some life-limited palliative care patients were asked their views about the list, they agreed with the losses, but the importance they placed on each loss varied enormously, and not only because of differences in age – one patient of eighty-nine was very concerned about his body image, which came as a surprise to some of the younger professional carers. A young amputee explained to me how difficult he found it when his reaction to his loss was different from what his parents, friends and, indeed, the hospital staff expected him to feel. He said, 'It was a bit awkward really, because they all thought I'd be terribly emotional, whereas by the time the leg came off I was relieved to be rid of the pain.'

This should alert us to the fact that experience of loss is unique to each individual and that our efforts to support will be effective only if we are careful not to make assumptions that the meaning of loss for a life-limited person may be very different from its meaning for us.

Look again at the list of losses and try to decide whether the list contains many items which would be equally true for the carer of a life-limited person.

I think you will agree that there are many similarities and that there may be some significant additional items. In the following case study try to identify the significant losses for the carer. Try also to relate these losses to the theories that we looked at earlier in the chapter.

Case study

Tessa and John have been married for eighteen years. They have known each other since school days and have some shared hobbies and friends, although each also has some separate activities. They have three children, fifteen, twelve and ten. John had two minor strokes, from which he made a very good recovery and, although changed, the family lifestyle has not been severely disrupted — Tessa has continued with her part-time job and John has returned to work, though with a slightly reduced work load. Against all expectation, John had a further major stroke which has left him severely disabled and with significant speech impairment. He is no longer completely continent and there seems to have been, in Tessa's words, 'Some sort of personality change — he's bad tempered and if I say anything he just laughs at me.' The children find their father's condition embarrassing and spend as much time away from home as possible. Tessa decided to give up her job to look after John; 'I married him for better or for worse. I just hope my health keeps up.'

Although some of Tessa's losses are paralleled by John's, I think you will agree that some are significantly different and that some of her anxieties may be significantly different too.

In terms of theory, Tessa's 'structures of meaning' have been overturned profoundly — the meanings of 'wife', 'mother' (core aspects of her personality) have undergone great change. 'Home' is no longer what it was, but is a place of sickness or a prison and presents worrying financial problems, as the mortgage repayments are high (on the assumption of John's career prospects) and maintenance is costly.

Her 'assumptive world' — that they would be, 'just a normal family' and that their children would grow to adulthood in this house and that then 'we'd have time for ourselves' — has been powerfully altered. John had been part of her life 'for as long as I can remember', but he now seems a different person and she sees this almost as a bereavement, with all the unhappiness of Bowlby's 'separation anxiety'.

Theories and models are of only academic interest unless they can enlighten us about how to help. It has been said that, 'There is nothing so practical as a good theory'. If we can use the theories to make our helping more effective, then their value becomes more than academic. Helping and communicating, or giving support, are two-way (at least) activities: the giver and the recipient. To be effective, helpers have to keep this dual process in mind and be as aware of their own need **to** support, as of the recipient's need **for** support. Touch is a good illustration of this: our compassion may mean that we would like to offer the comfort of touch, but how do we actually know that the other person wants or needs to be touched? The origin of the word 'theory' helps us to be aware of this two-way process. The Greek word *theoros*, when it is used as a noun, refers to an observation or an observer/onlooker. When it is used as a verb, it means to contemplate or observe. Theories of loss, can help us to be more astute observers of those we wish to help. The negative side is that we could become coldly analytical, and merely observe and categorise people according to theory. What could be less helpful than to tell someone like Tessa, in our case study, how she fits into a theory of loss? Knowledge of theory is a good foundation for understanding suffering, but translating that understanding into good practice which keeps the individual and the unique nature of the suffering firmly in mind, is vital. The theory should help us to be sensitive observers, but it is our active involvement and **use** of the theory which will make us effective helpers. The recipient will experience our help as sensitive because it is founded on understanding (whether she or he knows anything of the theory or not). The great Swiss philosopher and theorist Carl Jung said:

> *Learn your theories as well as you can, but put them*
> *aside when you touch the Miracle of the Living Soul.*
> *Not theories, but your own creative individuality*
> *must decide.*

This expresses well the dual nature of helping — theory is valuable and worthwhile spending time and effort on ('learn your theories as well as you can'). It gives us insight into how people experience loss and the impact that loss may have. At the same time in order to reach out and help, we must be aware of two things — the needs of the other (the 'living soul') and that we, too, are individuals and can be creative. The value of loss theory to palliative care is that it can, if we bear Jung's statement in mind, enlarge and enhance opportunities for helping.

To complete this chapter try to answer the following questions (perhaps using a journal or note book) based on your learning so far.

1. Bowlby, Marris and Murray-Parkes are all western Europeans. Do you consider that their theories may be limited?
2. What do you see as the significant difference between Marris's and MurrayParkes's theories (if any)?
3. Do the advantages of a knowledge of loss theory outweigh the disadvantages? How?
4. What contribution does loss theory make to palliative care?
5. Will your knowledge of loss help or change your helping practices? How?

References

Bowlby J (1969) *Attachment and Loss (Volume 1) Attachment*. Hogarth, London

Bowlby J (1972) *Attachment and Loss (Volume 2) Separation*. Hogarth, London

Bowlby J (1980) *Attachment and Loss: Separation — Anxiety and Anger*. Hogarth, London

Bowlby J (1982) *Loss: Sadness and Depression*. Hogarth, London

James N, Field D (1992) The routinisation of hospice: Bureaucracy and charismas, *Soc Sci Med* **34**: 12

Marris P (1974) *Loss and Change*. Routledge, London

Murray-Parkes CM (1986) *Bereavement: Studies of grief in adult life*. Pelican Books, London

2

Needs and wants

Think for a moment of a newborn baby. What do you think are his/her needs?

You might have listed:

- food
- shelter (in the sense of physical warmth and comfort)
- light and air
- safety (babies seem afraid of falling, and of loud noise even if it is harmless)

You might have added something like **'nurture'** particularly after reading about Bowlby's attachment theory in *Chapter 1*. **'Nurture'** implies more than physiological needs, and perhaps encompasses human touch or closeness.

The psychologist Abraham Maslow devised a hierarchy of human needs (*Figure 2.1*) (1962), which has become famous,

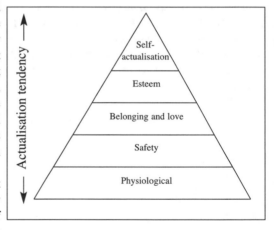

Figure 2.1: Maslow's Hierarchy of Human Needs (1962)

especially in humanistic thinking. This has been elaborated to take in further concepts (*Figure 2.2*).

Maslow considered that it is, in general, not possible to progress up the hierarchy unless the needs at the base of the pyramid are met. Do you agree? Sometimes, of course, exceptional people may ignore or suppress their more basic needs. Perhaps you can think of some examples? You might have considered people who sacrifice themselves for their beliefs, or who put others' needs before their own.

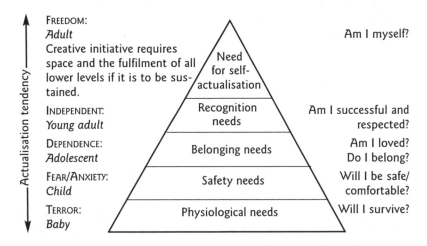

Figure 2.2: A variation on Maslow's pyramid

Returning to the needs of our neo-natal: we may agree about his or her needs, but how could we know what it **wants**? Generally speaking, the infant's carers decide that they know what it wants, because it communicates by crying. That is, the carers react from their own assumptions about what the crying means.

Little research has been done into whether there is a difference between what a baby needs and what it might want. Melanie Klein (Mitchell, 1986) is one of the few theorists who has attempted to explore the shadowy pre-speech internal world of babies. Her observations led her to think that babies are not passive reactors to their environment ('I am hungry', 'I am cold'), but are actively interacting with that environment, which includes the emotional environment. Her theories are often criticised because they are not testable – we cannot ask the babies for their views about what they want, as opposed to what they need. Are we in danger, sometimes, of making the same assumptions about life-limited people and their carers? Do we assume that we know what they need and therefore what they want? Yet the crucial difference is that the adults, unlike the babies, are able to communicate by more than crying. The crucial task for those of us who want to help is to elicit and listen to that communication.

Make a list of what you consider to be the needs of a dying person. Here are some possible areas that you might consider:

- physical needs
- privacy
- distraction(s)
- contact
- information
- decision making
- control.

If you have the opportunity, check your list with the views of someone who works with life-limited people.

Your list of needs will have come from your own observation or experience of what a dying person needs, or perhaps from what you imagine would be your own needs if you were reaching the terminal phase of an illness. Inevitably, there will be some assumptions, but would you agree that we have a responsibility to determine whether what we think a person needs corresponds with what they want?

Study the two following lists of the rights of dying people.

The dying person's Bill of Rights:

- I have the right to be treated as a living human being until I die.
- I have the right to maintain a sense of hopefulness, however changing its focus may be.
- I have the right to be cared for by those who can maintain a sense of hopefulness, however changing this might be.
- I have the right to express my feelings and emotions about my approaching death in my own way.
- I have the right to participate in decisions concerning my case.
- I have the right to expect continuing medical and nursing attention even though 'cure' goals must be changed to 'comfort' goals.
- I have the right not to die alone.
- I have the right to be free from pain.
- I have the right to have my questions answered honestly.
- I have the right not to be deceived.
- I have the right to have help from and for my family in accepting my death.
- I have the right to die in peace and dignity.

- I have the right to retain my individuality and not be judged for my decisions, which may be contrary to the beliefs of others.
- I have the right to discuss and enlarge my religious and/or spiritual experiences, regardless of what they may mean to others.
- I have the right to expect that the sanctity of the human body will be respected after death.
- I have the right to be cared for by caring, sensitive, knowledgeable people who will attempt to understand my needs and will be able to gain some satisfaction in helping me face my death.

Declaration of rights of people with cancer

This declaration of rights of people with cancer has been produced by CancerLink to bring the needs of people with cancer to the attention of health professionals, employers and the public at large.

The document is designed to act as a starting point for debate about how the needs of people with cancer are being met and how service provision could be improved.

The following do not all exist as legal rights but are felt to be fundamental to the well being of people with cancer.

I have the right:

- to equal concern and attention whatever my gender, race, class, culture, religious belief, age, sexuality, lifestyle or degree of able-bodiedness
- to be considered with respect and dignity, and to have my physical, emotional, spiritual, social and psychological needs taken seriously and responded to throughout my life, whatever my prognosis
- to know I have cancer, to be told in a sensitive manner and to share in all decision-making about my treatment and care in honest and informative discussions with relevant specialists and other health professionals
- to be informed fully about treatment options and to have explained to me the benefits, side-effects and risks of any treatment.
- to be asked for my informed consent before I am entered into any clinical trial
- to a second opinion, to refuse treatment or to use complementary therapies without prejudice to continued medical support

- to have any special welfare needs acknowledged and benefit claims responded to promptly
- to be employed, promoted or accepted on return to work according to my abilities and experience and not according to assumptions about my disease and its progression
- to easy access to information about local and national services, cancer support and self help groups and practitioners that may be useful in meeting my needs
- to receive support and information to help me understand and come to terms with my disease, and to receive similar support for my family and friends.

It would be interesting to know whether the lists were compiled by dying people themselves or by carers (professional or informal). What are your views about these 'rights'? Compare the 'rights' with your list of needs and try to decide whether the rights cover the needs you identified.

In its *Global Strategy of Health*, the World Health Organization (WHO) stated that by the year 2000:

> *Everyone should be afforded comfort and dignity at the time of death.*

We might agree that 'comfort' (a very broad term) and 'dignity' are highly desirable – at any time – but how can we establish what individual dying people want in addition to these broad aims for them? Look again at the two lists of 'rights'. Put a tick against those you agree with, and a cross against any you think are unrealistic or unreasonable. You may be left with some items about which you are unsure. If we think that many of the 'Rights' are reasonable, then we have to accept that someone – the carer, professional or informal – has a responsibility to meet the needs implied in the rights. How ready would you say that most carers are to take on the responsibility?

It may be that in accommodating 'rights' we have to consider the needs of carers, both professional and informal.

List what you think are these needs:
Informal:
Professional:

In a recent survey (Bayliss, 2001), informal carers were asked to prioritise some of their needs. Three items were consistently given a high priority:

⌘ Help to say 'goodbye' to the dying person.
⌘ Spiritual (not necessarily religious) help – particularly to wrestle with those 'why?' questions.
⌘ To be a real person ('not a carer or a nurse, but me').

Yet these had hardly been seen as needs by those who originally compiled the list of what they thought were informal carers' needs. Were they high on your list? This perhaps highlights how careful we need to be about assuming that we know what 'they' need.

Professional carers are assumed to have appropriate palliative care **skills** – although the majority of UK deaths occur in hospitals where training in palliative care may be limited. However, all care work can be stressful, despite its rewards, and the potential for burn out or for distancing when working intimately with the dying is considerable. Listen to this statement made by a Macmillan nurse during clinical supervision (and reproduced with her permission):

> *There seems to be some sort of belief that if you're a good professional you somehow mustn't or shouldn't have feelings – as if the uniform, or something, makes you immune. But if you've worked with a family through to the death of one of its most important members, how can you not have feelings? And having to go on putting a brave face on things gets to be exhausting, when you might have several deaths in a month.*

Palliative care is not only about appropriate nursing skills, but about providing a more holistic care; trying to meet the physical and emotional needs of both the patient and the informal carer(s) can be exhausting. Look back at your list of the needs of professional carers and reflect again on the professional's needs. It is probably true that we cannot meet the needs of others unless, or until, we know how to meet our own. Those of us working in the field of care frequently notice that many carers who are close to burnout, or even breakdown, seem unable to accept help and support — almost as if this would demean the quality of their care. Yet, I have seen carers become quite irritable when those they try to help seem determined to refuse it — one supervisee used the term, 'they acutally want to be martyrs'. We need to reflect, perhaps, that if we cannot accept support (which may come from non-managerial or clinical supervision) we are not as effective at providing it.

'Wants' and 'needs' then may be different, not only for patients and carers, but different from each other. Perhaps the strongest taboo around the terminally ill is the inability to be open about issues with the patient who wants to die. Everything possible may have been done to meet his or her perceived needs, but what the patient wants is an end to the struggle. Obituary notices frequently say things like 'after a long (or brave) fight with cancer', thus acknowledging that coping with a terminal illness can seem like a battle; and battles are exhausting. One life-limited patient, interviewed for this chapter, said that his most pressing need was, 'someone to give me permission to give up.' Many ethical questions are raised by trying to provide people with what they want – if that is death – as well as trying to meet their needs. The dilemma is expressed by the husband of Diane Pretty, a motor neurone sufferer, who took her 'right to die' to the High Court and to the European Court of Human Rights (notice his use of the word 'wants'):

> *... because we all love her, losing Diane will be devastating, but I have come to terms with what she wants and I have to respect her decision. If a doctor could agree to her request, we'd all be terribly upset, but we'd be pleased to know she had had the good death she wants, and not been forced to carry on when she feels her life is over.*

Clearly in the Pretty family, the topic was not taboo, but it can present a huge barrier to open communication, particularly if we are confused about our own views on this difficult and contentious ethical issue.

An attempt to resolve these questions is the 'living will' or 'advance directive'. These are attempts by dying people (or, indeed, by healthy people whose death does not seem imminent) to express not only the type of care they require should they become unable to express their choice, but also to state when they want that care to cease. These directives sometimes state explicitly, 'let me die when/if...' or, 'do not resuscitate me if...'. The legality of living wills is, at the time of writing, still controversial both in the UK and elsewhere, but there is increasing interest in the ethical issues associated with voluntary euthanasia, or assisted death, and a person's 'right to die'. Being clear about our own stance on this difficult subject is important, if we are to work and communicate with the dying. Here is an example of an advance directive;

when you have read it, think carefully about whether you could follow the directions if they had been given by someone for whom you are the prime carer (whether in a professional or informal capacity).

Living will declaration

To my family, doctors, and all those concerned with my care, I, ...being of sound mind, make this statement as a directive to be followed if for any reason I become unable to participate in decisions regarding my medical care.

I direct that life-sustaining procedures should be withheld or withdrawn if I have an illness, disease or injury, or experience extreme mental deterioration, such that there is no reasonable expectation of recovering or regaining a meaningful quality of life. These life-sustaining procedures that may be withheld or withdrawn include, but are not limited to:

Surgery   Antibiotics   Cardiac resuscitation   Respiratory support
Artificially administered feeding and fluids

I further direct that treatment be limited to comfort measures only, even if they shorten my life.

[You may delete any provision above by drawing a line through it and adding your initials.]

Other personal instructions:

These directions express my legal right to refuse treatment. Therefore, I expect my family, doctors, and all those concerned with my care to regard themselves as legally and morally bound to act in accord with my wishes, and in so doing to be free from any liability for having followed my directions.

Signed...Date......................

Witness..................................Witness..................................

Proxy designation clause

[If you wish, you may use this section to designate someone to make treatment decisions if you are unable to do so. Your Living Will Declaration will be in effect even if you have not designated a proxy.]

I authorise the following person to implement my Living Will Declaration by accepting, refusing and/or making decisions about treatment and hospitalisations:

Name………………………………………………..

Address……………………………………………………………..

If the person I have named above is unable to act on my behalf, I authorise the following person to do so:

Name………………………………………………..

Address……………………………………………………………..

I have discussed my wishes with these persons and trust their judgment on my behalf.

Signed………………………………………….Date……………….……

Witness…………………………….Witness………………………………

Advance directive

To my family, my physician and all other persons concerned this directive is made by me.

At a time when I am of sound mind and after careful consideration:

I DECLARE that if at any time the following circumstances exist, namely:

1. I suffer from one or more of the conditions mentioned in the schedule;
2. I have become unable to participate effectively in decisions about my medical care;
3. Two independent physicians (one a consultant) are of the opinion that I am unlikely to recover from illness or impairment involving severe distress or incapacity for rational existence.

THEN AND IN THOSE CIRCUMSTANCES my directions are as follows:

1. that I am not to be subjected to any medical intervention or treatment aimed at prolonging or sustaining my life;
2. that any distressing symptoms (including any caused by lack of food or fluid) are to be fully controlled by appropriate analgesic or other treatment, even though that treatment may shorten my life.

I consent to anything proposed to be done or omitted in compliance with the directions expressed above and absolve my medical attendants from any civil liability arising out of such acts or omissions.

I wish it to be understood that I fear degeneration and indignity far more than I fear death. I ask my medical attendants to bear this statement in mind when considering what my intentions would be in any uncertain situation.

I RESERVE the right to revoke this DIRECTIVE at any time, but unless I do so it should be taken to represent my continuing directions.

SCHEDULE

A. Advanced disseminated malignant disease
B. Severe immune deficiency
C. Advanced degenerative disease of the nervous systems.
D. Severe and lasting brain damage due to injury, stroke, disease or other cause.
E. Senile or pre-senile dementia, whether Alzheimer's, multi-infarct or other.
F. Any other condition of comparable gravity.

Signed..Date........................

WE TESTIFY that the above-named signed this Directive in our presence, and made it clear to us that he/she understood what it meant. We do not know of any pressure being brought on him/her to make such a directive and we believe it was made by his/her own wish. So far as we are aware we do not stand to gain from his/her death.

Witnessed by: ....

Issued by the Voluntary Euthanasia Society, 13 Prince of Wales Terrace, London, W8 5PG

> Would you want to write an advance directive or living will yourself? How might you feel if your directions were either ignored or in other, more subtle ways, not carried out?

Although the idea of the living will as a way of opening up the debate about choice and control in dying seems to be increasing, there are many concerns about whether it would help families, relatives, carers, health-care professionals in practice. It is interesting that their needs, or wants, have to be taken into consideration, as well as the choices of the dying person. Some of the difficulties which have been raised are in the following list. Think carefully about each and consider how they might apply to you. Think especially about the effects on communication:

- In the care of elderly people, there is often an existing Power of Attorney, where choice in health care (which may imply withdrawal of treatment) is given to another person.
- Accurate predictions about recovery are not always possible. As one carer put it to me, 'What if I agreed and the next day a cure was found?'
- The age of the person who makes a living will may present difficulties. Is a person of sixteen, for example, capable of making a valid choice? (In this connection, I was asked to work with a palliative care specialist who had followed the parents' wishes for a seventeen-year-old cancer patient. This involved much treatment and some invasive surgery. After the patient's death she discovered that the patient had made a living will, but the parents could not bring themselves to accede to what he wanted.)
- Healthcare professionals are concerned about the distinction between life-sustaining and life-saving treatment. Until this is clear, they think the choice must remain with the medical profession.

❋ A living will/advance directive would have to be regularly (perhaps annually) updated. The cost of this to doctors, or for solicitors, with whom a document would be lodged, could be prohibitive.

❋ There may be conflict (sometimes based on religious principles) between the writer of the living will and those required to carry out its directives; or between relatives themselves; or between relatives and professionals. The last thing a dying person may want is conflict around them.

The living will may therefore not help in practice (Gallagher, 1993), but we need to have thought through the issues if our communication is to be effective. The dilemma surrounding this topic is reflected in a newspaper correspondence in response to an article entitled 'How civilised are we if we refuse an easeful death?'

> My thanks to John Humphrys for raising the question of the right to death with dignity (Comment, last week).
>
> My mother was senile from the age of sixty-two to her death fifteen years later. I am determined not to suffer the same fate. As the law stands I can see no way of being sure of avoiding this other than to kill myself while I am still compos mentis not to botch the job, which seems a sad waste. If I could write a directive that in the event of my becoming senile in the opinion of, say, two doctors, I would be eased out of this life by the medical profession, I could heave a sigh of relief and get on with enjoying life.   Patricia Kaye, Polis, Cyprus.

> DUTY: Humphrys is wrong to suggest it is wrong to sentence people to a life they no longer want. As a hospice nurse my experience assures me that those who are dying invariably have as their prime concern those whom they love, not themselves. In this sense, as the eminent Dr Peter Kaye has suggested, 'the right to die' could become 'the duty to die'. To argue that it is an individual choice to die is largely false. Decisions are bound to be influenced by the needs perceived by the dying person of those whom they love. If euthanasia is an option then the dying patient may well feel duty-bound to opt for it. Instead of promoting euthanasia we should promote palliative care. The patient and family may enjoy what those in palliative care witness so often, that is, a positive end to a valued life allowing for reflection, sometimes reconciliation, preparation and time with people who matter.
>
> Denise James, Overstone, Northampton

NO WAY TO LIVE: Would we not all sleep better knowing that in the event that we did become terminally ill and were sure to suffer, we would have the choice to die peacefully? We shoot animals suffering from an injury that cannot be helped and we put down ageing animals that are suffering. The fact that it is not practical to create animal hospitals where they can be in a bed until they die a 'natural' death is not the point. The point is that suffering is no way to live the last days of our lives yet we reserve this privilege for our pets.

If suicide is now legal why on earth is euthanasia illegal?

Christie Harris, Taunton, Somerset

CHOICE: The sad fact is that until we, as a civilised society, allow the choice of self-deliverance, we are not a civilised society, we are an inhumane one.   Mary Fahy, Queensland, Australia

Sunday Times, 17 March 2002

Effective communication depends, to some extent, on good self-awareness. Elizabeth Kübler-Ross, the great pioneer of listening to the needs and wants of the dying, said:

> *It is essential that everyone caring for the dying and*
> *their families understands... their own concerns and*
> *anxieties in order to avoid a projection of their own*
> *fears.*

In other words, if we do not take the time and trouble to examine our 'concerns and anxieties', we will make assumptions about the needs and wants, not to mention the fears, of the people we are hoping to help. A research study (Heaven and Maguire, 1996) of nurses at two hospices looked at how training in communication skills did (or did not) help them to identify accurately their patients' concerns. Surprisingly, the nurses were unable to identify 60% of the concerns. Here are the difficulties which the study found. Do some of them resonate with your own anxieties?

⌘ Sharing and disclosing feelings may not be in the patient's best interest.
⌘ If the dying person becomes distressed or angry it may be very difficult to regain control of a situation.

⌘ It may not be ethical or useful to allow to the surface anxieties or concerns about which nothing can be done. It may therefore be in everyone's best interest to block their surfacing as this reduces distress for everyone.

⌘ There may be a lack of clarity about what patients know about their illness and this creates fears about being unable to answer questions, which in turn inhibits communication.

⌘ The emotional cost of 'getting too close' to a patient (often seen as unprofessional, too) inhibits interactions.

Those conducting the survey conclude:

> *It is... ironic that, in trying to offer support to patients, nurses are blocking the disclosure of emotions and concerns, which is fundamental to providing that help and benefit which they seek to offer.*

When Kübler-Ross urged us to be aware of our own concerns and anxieties she was, in part, talking about the concerns and anxieties we have in relation to our own mortality. Several attempts have been made to determine or to 'scale' people's fear of dying. One of the few large-scale surveys about attitudes and beliefs about death and dying (and there was little attempt to separate the two) was carried out in Italy. Look at the results and reflect on whether they resonate with what you feel or would expect others to feel (*Tables 2.1* and *2.2*).

Table 2.1: Do you ever think about death?	
	per cent
Always	5.8
Often	22.1
Sometimes	44.3
Rarely/never	27.3

It is interesting that in *Table 2.3* the strongest response is of loss — their own and of leaving loved ones. This perhaps confirms some of Bowlby's theory about separation which we looked at in *Chapter 1*. A criticism of these questionnaires, of course, is that we cannot realistically predict our fears until we reach a stage where death is a real possibility or an imminent certainty, rather than an abstract concept that, 'all living thing die'. Even so, thinking carefully about our possible or probable fears may develop the self-awareness vital for good communication. An example of a possible list of fears is given at the end of this chapter, but you are urged not to complete it when you feel fragile or have no one with whom to talk it over.

Table 2.2: What is your main feeling when you think about your own death and dying?

	per cent
Fear	25.7[a]
Great sadness	20.0[b]
resignation	17.8
Serenity	8.5[c]
Indifference	5.5
Curiosity	3.3
I don't think about it	13.0
Other	3.5
Don't know/can't answer	2.7
[a] people less than twenty-four years	29–33
[b] people fifty-five to sixty-four years old	23
[c] people more than sixty years old	15

Table 2.3: What bothers you most when you think about death?

	per cent
The sadness of leaving life and loved ones	50.9[a]
The idea of no longer being there, that it's the end, just 'nothingness'	22.1
Thoughts about what will happen after	9.8
Nothing in particular	11.3
Other	1.8
Don't know/can't answer	4.1
I don't think about it	13.0
Other	3.5
[a] women	54
[b] people more than forty-five years old	54

In the counselling field, self-awareness has always been seen as a crucial quality. Our own personal experiences of deaths and bereavement will certainly influence our interactions, but awareness will make us cautious about assuming that these experiences necessarily result in the same feelings in others. Dying people and their relatives will evoke the normal range of emotions — we will like some and feel negative about others — and being honest with ourselves about this range and acknowledging the negative as well as the positive is an important step towards self-awareness. It can have added bonuses too — some patients feel unable to express their own negative feelings if they perceive their helper as some kind of saint who never experiences anything but good, kind, compassionate emotions! Monitoring success in communication and measuring where we feel we did not overcome obstacles is a good route to avoiding the blocking which was found in the survey. Being professional does not mean being impersonal; being close to dying people and their relatives is rewarding; it becomes unprofessional only if we **over** identify.

We also need to develop awareness of how we feel if our attempts are rejected. Communicating with compliant, appreciative people (whatever their prognosis) is easier than working with 'difficult' people. Being aware of our own biases and anxieties about rejection or aggression can help ensure that we continue to give quality care.

This chapter closes with a witness statement from a hospice volunteer, which perhaps sums up the points made in this chapter.

> *I came to help in the hospice because my mother died here and I thought I'd like to 'give a bit back'. Also, having nursed her at home for a while and then here, I thought I knew everything about the business of dying. How wrong can you be?! Everyone is different – no two people have the same needs. And I have to tell you that I had a lot to learn about myself. If it hadn't been for team support I'd have lost patience or lost heart or something. I'm much clearer now about my attitudes to all sorts of things and about what **real** communication means, even silence, especially if that's what's wanted.*

This list of 'fears' was compiled from a sample of people, none of whom had a terminal diagnosis or a life-threatening illness. Whether we find the list shocking, surprising, or 'too close to home' does not, in a sense, matter. In terms of self-awareness the issue is whether, firstly, we could ensure that the fears could be communicated by facilitating expression, and, if expressed, that we could work with them.

What frightens me about my own dying is:

- losing control
- losing my intellectual capacities
- being left alone
- being a burden
- that my death will not be witnessed
- being looked down upon
- the pain
- getting weak
- that I will be hooked to machines and gadgets
- being emotionally overwhelmed
- not knowing what's going on
- getting inadequate medical care
- being declared dead when I'm still alive
- being buried alive
- being isolated from others
- that I will die of cancer
- looking ugly
- the grief I would cause my relatives and friends
- dying too slowly
- being unable to die calmly
- dying too soon
- being too weak to say goodbye to my loved ones
- that the nurses will not realise when it happens
- being in agony
- that I may act disgracefully
- that I will die in a fire
- that I will suffocate
- that I will be murdered.

To check your knowledge and understanding of this chapter, try to answer the following questions.

1. Where would you see yourself as mostly living on the Maslow hierarchy? Where would you place a life-limited person on the hierarchy? How could you check?
2. What skills are needed to elicit the wants and needs of palliative care patients?
3. Why is it important to be aware of the wants and needs of carers as well as those of the patient?

4. Even if you agree with some of the points made about living wills, try to formulate a reasoned response to each difficulty
5. On a scale of 1 to 10 where would you place yourself in terms of awareness bearing in mind the 'blocking' described in the Heaven and Maguire study?

References

Bayliss J (2001) *Needs of Carers of the Terminally Ill*. Unpublished

Gallager U (1993) The living will in clinical practice. In: Dickenson D Johnson M, eds. *Death, Dying and Bereavement*. Oxford University Press with Sage Publications, London

Heaven C, Maguire P (1998) Blocking out emotions. *J Adv Nurs* **23**(2): 280–6

Kübler-Ross E (1970) *On Death and Dying*. Tavistock, London

Maslow AH (1962) *Toward a Psychology of Being*. Princeton Reinhold

Mitchell J (1986) *The Selected Melanie Klein*. Penguin, Harmondsworth

Southwestern Michigan Inservice Education Council, quoted in 'Ann Landers' syndicated newspaper column, 1978

Toscani F *et al* (1991) Death and Dying, Perceptives and Attitudes in Italy. *Palliative Medical* **5**: 334–43

Sunday Times (2002) How civilised are we if we refuse an easeful death? *Sunday Times*: 10 March

3

Sustaining hope

In the Christian canon, hope is one of the great trio of virtues, along with faith and love, the latter being the 'greatest' of the three. In the research for this chapter, it became very clear that although hope means different things to different people (sometimes radically different), it is an important factor in day-to-day life, and a word that is used with considerable frequency. The English language is full of sayings, or quotations, whose authors are no longer connected with the quotations, about hope. Take a minute or two to scribble down the sayings you can recall about hope.

Two of the most commonly known are:

> *Where there's life there's hope.*
> *Hope springs eternal in the human breast.*

For a dying person and his or her relatives or carers, how true do you think either of these sayings is?

The first quotation, from the poet John Gay's *Fables*, is part of a dialogue between a sick man and an angel. The sick man asserts that as long as he can draw breath he can hope to stay alive. In the poem, this seems to be all that he is hoping for — to stay alive. In palliative care, we know that hope is much more complex than this, but if we are to work more with Pope's assertion that 'Hope springs eternal in the human breast', we need to clarify what the terminally ill person and his or her carers (both formal and informal) are hoping for.

A popular exercise on training courses is the time-line: trainees are asked to mark on a line significant events which marked a turning point in their lives. Or, they might to be asked to mark significant losses or bereavements. The exercise is usually helpful in increasing self-awareness; it is often surprising to reflect on how many losses one has survived.

> It is rare, however, to see this exercise used for hope, but you might like to try it for yourself and to reflect on the changing nature of your hopes from childhood to whatever age you are now.

Here are two statements by two palliative care patients:

When I was young I suppose I hoped for fairly straightforward things — nice home, good partner, healthy children, — you know, just the usual things. I don't think I actually hoped for good health, I just took it for granted. When my father got dementia, I suppose I hoped I wouldn't get like him... . Then, when I got cancer, at first I hoped it would go away, or that there was some mistake or that there'd be a cure or something. Then I went through a ridiculous phase when I kept saying, 'If I can just keep going until...', it might have been the holidays, or Fred's retirement, anything really. I don't know what I expected to happen, it was silly really. Now?... It's difficult to say, really. I try to take each day as it comes and hope that there won't be any pain or that I'll have some visitors and won't be too weary to see them... . I hope I'm not a burden to anyone... .

It's hard to talk about hope, because I don't really know what it means anymore. When I was first diagnosed I think I hoped for small, day-to-day things like seeing the roses in the garden or that I'd get to the end of a book, which probably sounds trivial. Now?... I suppose if I'm honest I hope for a decent end. Not that I want to die, exactly, but since I know that I'm going to, I hope that it will be OK... though what I mean by that I'd find it hard to tell you!

Several points about hope can be gleaned from these two patients, which may help us both in terms of self-awareness and in terms of communication.

The first patient's hope seems to have demonstrated some of the stages of dying, described by Elizabeth Kübler-Ross (1970). Kübler-Ross was a pioneer in putting the emotional needs of dying people and their families at the forefront of terminal care and her stages model of dying has been very influential. It is not without its critics, but is a useful starting point for considering where hope may usefully be explored as a coping strategy. Kübler-Ross's five stages are:

Denial

The person cannot accept that a terminal diagnosis has been made. The denial may manifest itself in a variety of ways – such as seeking second (or third and fourth) opinions or looking, often frantically, for 'cures'.

Anger

After the initial shock, the growing realisation brings anger or even rage and fury, which may be directed against the medical profession, family, God. It is as if someone or something must be blamed for what is happening.

Bargaining

After anger, the dying person attempts some kind of 'deal' with fate (sometimes in the guise of the medical profession) or God. The 'deal' is usually that they be allowed to live until some significant event is achieved – the arrival of a new baby or a family wedding, for instance. The dying person's side of the bargain is not clear, but may sometimes be expressed in terms like, 'I'll die peacefully if...'.

Depression

As the illness progresses and the realisation that neither angry protests nor bargaining will change things and as hope of recovery diminishes, depression sets in. As with most depressions, there is likely to be withdrawal, with strong feelings of unworthiness and a fear of dying which may or may not be expressed overtly.

Acceptance

The patient gives up the struggle and begins to let go, which results in a lifting of the depression. Even so, acceptance does not necessarily mean happy reconciliation with the unavoidable; indeed, the stage may be characterised by an absence of feeling.

> What do you think might be some of the criticisms of this model (which is sometimes used to trace stages of bereavement, as well as of dying).

Here are some of the doubts which have been raised. It is only fair to point out that some problems with the model may have more to do with those who follow it too rigidly, than with Kübler-Ross's own thinking.

It is sometimes said that people don't 'progress' to acceptance, as if the stages are some sort of route towards a 'good' death, because 'progress' implies sound, commendable effort. It is also sometimes said that people 'get stuck' in one or other of the stages, with the implication that they should 'move on', but if they gain comfort, hope or just coping mechanisms, by being 'stuck' maybe there is no need to 'move on'. It is unlikely that Kübler-Ross would have taken this slightly judgemental approach, but I have myself heard some palliative care workers criticised because 'they aren't getting them through to acceptance'. Denial may be a valuable defence for some people, and removing defences can be risky.

Denial

There are implications here for hope. Our first patient seemed, at some point to have been in Kübler-Ross's first stage of **denial**: she found it difficult to accept the reality of her diagnosis. If her carers had tried to push her to 'progress' beyond this stage, might it have denied her the hope she needed to cope with the shock of the bad news, or the will to accept chemotherapy? The term 'in denial' is frequently used rather disapprovingly, when maybe being 'in denial' is what allows the patient to have hope.

(What is your view?)

Another problem with a stages model is that the carers or relatives of the dying person may want to stay 'in denial' because this allows **them** to hope, when the ill person may be at some other 'stage'. Unfortunate conflict can be the result.

Anger

Neither of our patients recalls feeling **angry**. (In the full initial interviews they were asked about this, but could recall only sadness and despair.) This is not to say that some life-limited people and their relatives do not experience anger, but it does challenge the idea that anger is a universal reaction. Providers of care may justifiably hope that anger may not be manifested, as it can sometimes be a difficult emotion to work with. The professional palliative carer can sometimes be caught between the anger of relatives, whose anger may well be on behalf of the patient as well as for themselves, and the calmer approach of the patient. It is difficult not to assume that because we feel angry about something, others don't feel it too. The anger of both patient and relatives may well be because the professional carer is not offering unrealistic hope; irrational though this may seem. A dying person and his or her relatives may be so desperate for hope, that they resent the professional who, in all honesty, cannot offer the sort of hope they require. This is not, however, to say that when anger is present it is impossible to bring hope – just that it is difficult.

> Pause for a moment and think how you might respond if you were the object of anger, or if you were trying to provide palliative care for a very angry person or his/her angry relatives. How could you bring hope into the emotional climate, to ameliorate and comfort, without being unrealistic.

Difficult isn't it? Good responses will depend on awareness that the anger, although it may be directed at us, does not have to be accepted as belonging to us. We also need good self-awareness that we are not colluding with the anger and being angry ourselves on behalf of the patient and/or family. Attempting to bring hope will depend very much on what our hopes are for the patient and this, in turn, will depend upon awareness of wants and needs. One hope that we may have is that we can use the anger. Anger, because it often manifests unpleasantly, is usually seen as negative, but it is often a great energising force and can be used positively.

Bargaining

Although our first patient seems to have experienced some of Kübler-Ross's third stage (although in the patient's case it was not third), she seems to have known that it was not very realistic, she calls it 'ridiculous' and 'silly'. Would you see bargaining as some sort of way of sustaining hope? If we know that the hope is not realistic, what sort of hope can we offer in its place? Relatives may be especially prone to bargaining. Two examples have been given to me by consultants:

> *If you cure him (of motor neurone disease) I promise*
> *I'll never speak another unkind word.*

> *Can you just keep her going until our daughter gets*
> *here from New Zealand — then I promise I'll let her*
> *go without any trouble?*

Clearly this kind of bargaining disguises some kind of hope and reflects the two quotations with which we began this chapter. For the palliative carer a more pertinent quotation might be:

> *Life's short span forbids us to enter on far-reaching*
> *hopes.*   (Horace)

The poet was reflecting on the shortness of life in general, but for those working with the life-limited there could be a useful lesson here – we should perhaps forbid ourselves from entering into far-reaching hopes and concentrate on trying to fulfil more achievable hopes. Both our patients seem to express short-term hopes and our role is to help with these.

Depression

Indicators for depression are notoriously difficult to determine. It would be surprising if the mood of life-limited people and those who care about and care for them were not sad. The losses they are experiencing and the possible fears – of pain or of death itself – the anxieties which could range from financial to existential, all make it likely that some form of depression would exist. Social withdrawal is also sometimes seen as a symptom of depression and this may, in palliative care, be more to do with the withdrawal of others. Many people are embarrassed by illness of any kind and if they know that the prognosis is not good find it difficult to communicate. As one patient said, 'If they can't tell you to get well soon or that they hope you'll get better, they don't seem to know what to say'. There would seem to be grounds for expecting depression, but whether it comes as a fourth stage in a process is much more contentious. Our patients seem to have experienced sadness, but not in the suggested order. There is also good evidence that some people remain buoyant to the end, and have talked about a 'gift of life' as if the shortening of their life expectancy has somehow made them value life much more. Clearly, such people maintain hope. What would you say is their hope?

You may have felt that the hope lies in being able to make the most of each remaining day. Certainly, our second patient sees enjoying small things as pleasurable. The first patient seems less buoyant and her hope not to be a burden sounds rather sad and might possibly be taken for depression.

Bringing hope to the depressed is especially difficult, as the depression may have many layers. It is here that trying to establish wants and needs can be very helpful, since if we can attend to these then the patient can see some hopes fulfilled. Establishing the wants and needs is reliant on good communication and this is why counselling skills are vital in palliative care.

Acceptance

The final stage of the Kübler-Ross model is 'acceptance' — a word which occurs frequently in the literature associated with dying and, especially, bereavement. Usually the word seems to be used with overtones of approval, as if acceptance (the direct opposite of denial) is a good thing.

> Take a moment to focus your ideas about acceptance. Ask yourself what it might mean for a palliative care patient and those closest to him or her. Ask yourself what it means for you and especially whether acceptance could mean, as yet another poet (John Milton) put it: '... farewell Hope'.

Both our patients seem to be accepting, in the sense that they appear to acknowledge that their death is inevitable, but each still has hope. The first person hopes that she will not be a burden, and the second that he will have 'a decent end', even though he can't be precise about what that could be. For the palliative carer there is good opportunity here to bring hope, especially if we are able to help patients articulate what they see as a 'good' death and, once again, we can appreciate the need for sensitive communication, using counselling skills to facilitate that communication.

The concept of a 'good' death comes to us from a variety of influences: literature, personal experience, anecdote, our own wishes and many more. Try to describe what you would hope for as a good death, firstly for yourself and then for those you love. (This is not an easy task, and you may want to pause for a while if you find it upsetting.)

Elsewhere (Bayliss, 1996; Nyatanga, 2001) I have suggested that it is possible to view a 'good' death in three ways:

- medically
- naturally
- religiously or culturally.

A **medically good death** could be seen as one where the patient is kept alive for as long as possible. In 2002 there was a crucial legal decision allowing a woman (Miss B) who was paralysed from the neck down, but mentally competent, to refuse the treatment which was keeping her alive. Her doctors had opposed her wishes, which suggests that withdrawing treatment is not seen by some in the medical profession as a good death. Yet the patient's determination to fight that view indicates clearly her interpretation was very different. For palliative carers, a medically good death may mean very effective pain control. Most UK deaths take place in hospitals, where knowledge of palliative care may be limited and pain control may mean heavy sedation. If this is the case, who is the medically good death good for?

A **naturally good death** could encompass the ageing process or heart attacks. The former are often thought of as acceptable because they seem to be part of the natural life cycle. Heart attacks or fatal strokes are seen as 'good' because they are a speedy death, without long periods of pain or treatment and phrases like, 'a wonderful way to go' are often used. If, however, the person's belief system required certain rituals or practices to be carried out before death, would sudden and unexpected death be 'good'? Similarly, with death in old age which is often seen as in the natural order of things and summed up in terms like 'a good innings', the diseases of old age such as arthritis, dementia or other debilitating conditions may mean that for the dying person their death is not 'good'. For relatives, witnessing the distressing aspects of some forms of dementia can seem like a fearful end, rather than a good one. The term 'happy release' may apply more to the relatives than to the demented person.

Religious or cultural good death

Some people have a strong faith in an after life and believe that for their souls to rest or for their loved ones to mourn appropriately, certain tasks or rituals must be completed before death. For them, a good death involves preparation and readiness; sudden death would not seem good to them. People without a formal religious belief system sometimes feel strongly that they wish, regardless of possible pain, to be alert until the end. As one patient poignantly put it, 'I want to know when I go through that door'. Heavy sedation would not be seen as good by these people.

The notion of a 'good death' is very complex and if we are to fulfil patients' hopes of a good death, we need very fine communication skills to find out the individual hopes, and good self-awareness to avoid assuming that what we see as a 'good death' is necessarily what the patient sees. Being alert to our own fears will help us not to project.

Kübler-Ross's model has gained considerable currency in palliative care, but Weisman's model (1984) of an **appropriate death** may be more useful in terms of using counselling skills in palliative care, because it requires first class communication skills. Weisman's model (1972), unlike Kübler-Ross's, is not linear, it does not see a dying person as moving along a pathway with defined 'milestones' (even though Kübler-Ross herself would hardly have expected patients to comply and march obligingly along such a pathway), but is based more on Pattisons's view (1978):

> *I find no evidence to support specific stages of dying. Rather, dying patients demonstrate a wide variety of emotions that ebb and flow throughout our entire life as we face conflicts and crises...*
>
> *Rather, I suggest that our task is to determine the stresses and crises at a specific time, to respond to the emotions generated by that issue, and, in essence, to respond to where the patient is at in his or her living-dying.*

Weisman's 'appropriate death', which demands the response advocated by Pattison, has four components:

- reducing, but not necessarily eliminating, conflict
- making dying and death compatible with the dying person's self-image
- preserving or restoring relationships as much as possible
- fulfilling some of the dying person's expressed aims.

A striking feature of this model is that it is not prescriptive; it is realistic in acknowledging that all conflict may not be eliminated, that relationships can be restored as much as possible. Would you see its aims as providing opportunities for hope?

⌘ Conflict around a dying person can be of many sorts – between relatives, between relatives and professionals and between the dying person and all of this. The palliative carer who sees reducing conflict as hopeful needs good skills.

⌘ Even greater skill is needed to establish what the persons' self-image is. Do they see themselves as strong? Has parenting always been important to their self-esteem? How crucial was being self-reliant to their sense of self-worth? These are the areas that we need to explore with real sensitivity if we are to help with an 'appropriate' death.

⌘ Relationships, even or perhaps especially bad ones, are profoundly important throughout life. If we consider a dying person to be a living person, relationships will continue to be important. It is rewarding to enable the preservation of relationships and this may be a great bonus of enabling people to die at home. There is a difference between dying as father, mother, husband, wife, partner and dying as the patient in Ward 10.

⌘ To fulfil expressed aims, we have to use skills to find out what these aims are and remind ourselves that Weisman does not suggest that we can fulfil all, but *some* of them. Just as with wants and needs, we can bring hope, but at the same time be realistic about which aims we can fulfil.

> Go through each item of Weisman's model again and try to think of examples of how a carer could use hope as the underpinning principle for achieving an 'appropriate' death. Be as specific as you can.

The term 'quality of life' has a variety of meanings. It is frequently used in association with material comforts: a good quality of life often meaning financial security, a pleasant home, interesting holidays and so on.

> What are the defining characteristics for your personal 'quality of life'?

Were any of the points to do with material aspects (comfortable home, for example) or were most to do with more abstract things? Part of the National Council For Hospices and Specialist Palliative Care Services definition of palliative care (*Chapter 4*) says that its 'goal must be the best quality of life' for patients and their families. (It is interesting that it is quality of life which is the goal, rather than a 'good' death.)

Look back at your lists of wants and needs, and reflect on which of them would help the goal of 'best quality of life' for the palliative care patient and his/her family. Certainly, some 'material' aspects will help – adequate financial support, good pain control, pleasant surroundings for instance will all be important. Yet these may all be part of a more important aspect – peace of mind. For patients and their families what constitutes peace of mind will vary enormously, the task of the palliative care team is to communicate sensitively in order to find out just what does constitute peace of mind and aim – as far as possible – to achieve it so that we can say:

> *... today he put forth*
> *The tender leaves of hope.*
> William Shakespeare, *Henry VIII,* III, ii

To check your understanding of the points made in *Chapter 3*, try to answer the following questions:

1. Do you think it is realistic to use hope as an intervention in palliative care? Why/Why not?
2. Is it possible to balance hope and realism? How difficult is it? In what way(s)?
3. What do you see as the dangers in a linear (stages) model of dying?
4. If 'acceptance', the final stage of the Kübler-Ross model of dying, is seen as desirable, does this preclude hope? Why/Why not?
5. What do you see as the difference between a 'good' death and an 'appropriate' death?

References:

Bayliss J (1996) *Understanding loss and grief.* In: Nyatanga B, ed. *Why is it so Difficult To Die?* MA Healthcare Limited, Dinton, Salisbury

Kübler-Ross E (1970) *On Death and Dying.* Tavistock, London

Kübler-Ross E (1975) *Death: The Final Stage Of Growth.* Prentice Hall, New York

Pattison EM (1978) *The Living-dying Process.* McGraw Hill, New York

Weisman A (1972; 1984) *On Dying and Denying.* Behavioural Publications, New York

Weisman A (1989) *The Coping Capacity: On the nature of being mortal.* Human Sciences Press, New York

4

Palliative care and holistic communication

The advancement of medicine, both in terms of drugs and technology, in the nineteenth century led to what has been called the 'medicalisation of death', and a view that death is somehow a 'failure' rather than the natural end of what is a limited process – life. Since the mid-twentieth century, and especially with the growth of the hospice movement, there has been an acknowledgement that traditional 'treatment' is not completely meeting the needs of dying people. The speciality of palliative care grew from this acknowledgement. Originally, the principles of palliative care were applied only to terminally ill people, often thought to mean patients with cancer.

> Take a moment to write down your own definition of 'terminally ill'.

Here is one definition:

> *The terminal patient has been defined as one in whom, following accurate diagnosis, the advent of death is certain and not too far distant and for whom treatment has changed from the curative to the palliative.*
>
> (Griffin, 1991)

This definition seems to have five components. Does your personal definition also cover these points?

1. An accurate diagnosis has been made.
2. Cure is not possible.
3. The illness/disease is or will be progressive.
4. The timing of the death is not exact, but is 'not too far distant'.
5. Treatment will be for relief rather than for cure.

Palliative care often seems to be linked with cancer, yet many illnesses would meet the five criteria and hence benefit from palliative care.

> Perhaps you can list some.

My list would include:

- people with cardiac or respiratory failure
- multiple sclerosis
- AIDS
- motor neurone disease
- elderly people (with or without Alzheimer's/dementia).

Palliative **medicine** was created by the Royal College of Physicians, and the speciality aimed to incorporate psychological, social and spiritual aspects of terminal illness into a **medical** model. Palliative **care** emerged alongside the medical model in the late 1980s and aimed to apply its principles not only to dying people. There still seems to be some confusion about the meanings of palliative care, terminal care and hospice care, with the terms often used, it seems, interchangeably. Here is a statement from the National Council for Hospice and Specialist Palliative Care Services (1992):

> *Palliative care, as the World Health Organization has recognised, is the active, total care of patients whose disease no longer responds to curative treatment, and for whom the goal must be the best quality of life for them and their families.*
>
> *Palliative care is now a distinct medical speciality in the United Kingdom. It focuses on controlling pain and other symptoms, easing suffering and enhancing the life that remains. It integrates the psychological and spiritual aspects of care, to enable patients to live out their lives with dignity, as well as offering support to families both during the patient's illness and their bereavement. It offers a unique combination of care in hospices and at home. The support palliative care offers is often needed early on in the illness.*
>
> *In itself, palliative care neither hastens nor postpones death. It recognizes a patient's right to spend as much time at home as possible and pays equal attention to physical, psychological, social and spiritual aspects of care wherever the patient is.*
>
> *In its modern form hospice care developed in Britain, where it found a strong community and*

> *voluntary response, forged close links with the*
> *National Health Service and has begun to exert a*
> *significant influence on conventional medicine.*

For helpers, both professional and informal, it is perhaps important to acknowledge that the principles of palliative care need not be restricted to hospice provision. Indeed, many hospices see part of their function as educative, in order to spread the principles to a wider range of settings. You may be able to think of examples where palliative care is used outside a hospice environment.

Macmillan and Marie Curie nursing sometimes operate outside hospice ambience, and palliative care principles are spreading to more hospitals.

> Look again at the statement from the National Council; then try to list what these 'principles' might be.

You might have included any of these:

- promoting physical well-being (ie. health care)
- promoting psycho-social well-being
- emphasising quality of life
- an holistic approach
- involvement of significant people (partners, family)
- respect for patient autonomy
- open communication
- acknowledgment of a spiritual dimension.

This list would encompass a range of interventions and treatments which relieve symptoms or improve that elusive item 'quality of life', but it would be accepted that the interventions are not curative. There is an implication that a multi-skilled, multi-professional team will be required to provide all the care outlined on the list.

Discussion of palliative care and hospice care often, or nearly always, brings up the word 'holistic' — caring for the whole person. The 'whole person' is a very broad term, and covers physical, emotional/ psychological, cognitive and spiritual needs (and, as we have seen, the needs can vary considerably).

In this book we are concerned especially with communication, and with communication using counselling skills.

> Take some time to consider whether it is possible to communicate with the 'whole person'.

In his interesting paper *Bereavement and Biography* (1996), Tony Walter describes how the funerals of two people he knew (or perhaps thought he knew) well, opened up areas where he had no real experience of the person at all. If we think of people to whom we are closest this becomes, in a way, quite obvious. I have experienced my parents as a daughter, and observed them as grandparents, but I have no knowledge of how they were perceived as employees, or managers, and only partial knowledge of how they were experienced as brother and sister, and so on. Reflect for a moment on the extent to which you know the 'whole person' you think of as closest to you.

I think you will agree that fulfilling the holistic ideals of palliative care presents a major challenge, and that effective communication is a large part of that challenge. Thus, a carer has the individual challenge of balancing idealism and realism. This balancing — attempting holistic care, whilst acknowledging that total communication is unrealistic — is very demanding and, as we have seen, not always achieved. To sustain the balance, many qualities will be needed and some will be essential.

> What **qualities** would you want in a personal carer? Remember that here we are looking at communication, rather than at practical or medical skills, which are, of course, invaluable.

A great deal of research has been done into what qualities need to be present if the person being helped is to perceive a conversation or interview as worthwhile. Whilst many qualities are seen as desirable, three are seen as essential. These three have come to be called, 'the core conditions'.

Look up the word 'core' in a good dictionary, and you will find that its 'root' is the Latin word for 'heart'. The qualities, then, are at the heart of engaging inter-personally whether we are professional or informal carers.

These three qualities are:

Empathy

Sometimes called empathic understanding.

Acceptance

Also called unconditional positive regard, or non-possessive warmth, or respect.

Sincerity

Sometimes called genuineness or congruence.

Various explanations of these three qualities have been given. Before we explore their meanings, take time to write down your own definition of each quality.

> Empathy
> Acceptance
> Sincerity

Empathy

Carl Rogers, who developed the person-centred approach to counselling, defined empathy as (1967):

> *The ability to experience another person's world as*
> *if it were one's own, without losing the 'as if'.*

The last five words of Rogers's definition are very important, but are often the neglected part. In a sense, it would be disrespectful to imagine that we could actually experience someone else's world. We each have an individual point of view, and we experience life from a history encompassing a host of experiences and influences.

> Try watching a film or 'soap' with another person. If you can, do the same thing with someone from another culture. Then compare your impressions with theirs.

However similar our reactions to events may be, we will always be looking at the other person's feeling **as if** they were our own. The danger is if we assume that the other person's feelings and thoughts will be the same as ours: the often used, 'I know just how you feel, because...' is a good example of **not** being empathic. What the person hearing these words may think (but usually be too polite to say) is, 'How can you know how I feel? You aren't old/young; black/white; dying...'.

The use of 'must' may also indicate an assumption or a lack of empathy. 'The loss must have been devastating for you' — it will be a brave client who will respond, 'Well no, actually, it was a relief'. What the use of 'must' so often implies is, '**I** would find this devastating/ sad/embarrassing/etc. so you must...'.

Read this case material by a Macmillan nurse:

> I'm working now with a family where their eighteen-year-old son is the patient. It's a sad family because they lost his younger sister in an accident about six years ago. You'd never believe how differently the mother and father are taking it; even though they're both losing a son, and you'd perhaps expect them to react in a much the same way. But she's really angry and talks a lot about suing people, but he's very depressed and only talks about how he's let him (the son) down.

This perhaps reminds us of how dangerous it can be to make assumptions. Maybe, as you read the statement, you were checking what you predicted might be each parent's reaction? Empathy is not thinking that we can actually experience another's distress or feel their pain. It is more to do with listening for and trying to understand the other person's point of view (even if we find it distorted or even bizarre). Another aspect of Carl Rogers's '*as if*' is that if we become too entangled in what we imagine a person may be thinking or feeling, we lose some of the ability to help. Sympathy and empathy are not the same, as the following anecdote (which may be familiar to you) illustrates:

> A person has fallen into a river and is struggling.
>
> Person one comes along on a bicycle, sees the problem accurately, and calls, 'Hang on; I'll go and get help'.
>
> Person two then arrives and, seeing the struggles, jumps off the bicycle and calling, 'You poor thing! That must be terrible for you! Hang on — I'm coming to help you,' dives into the river. The water is deeper and colder than anticipated and the rescuer is not the strongest of swimmers.
>
> Person three assesses the problem and goes down to the river bank. Carefully and firmly planting one foot on the bank, s/he puts the other foot in the water and reaches out a saving hand.

Keeping 'one foot on the bank' is a crucial aspect of empathy and is what Rogers meant by 'without losing the as if'.

Acceptance

Empathy is closely linked to the second core quality of acceptance, because it involves respect. When we are trying 'to experience another person's world as if it were one's own, without losing the "as if" ', we may find that that world seems very alien to our point of view. It is hard to be accepting of a point of view, when you don't agree with it and maybe don't even understand it. The difficulty seems to have arisen partly because 'acceptance' has become confused with 'approval'; but, listening for and hearing another person's point of view doesn't necessarily mean that we have to approve it. What it does mean is that we respect that what a person is thinking and feeling is real for them. Gerard Egan (1999) (whose model of skilled helping is very popular) says that respect is:

> *An attitude or a moral quality, a way of looking at*
> *and prizing people.*

He suggests that we communicate respect by giving people our full attention, by striving to understand them and by believing that they have the potential to take responsibility for themselves and for their decisions. In general conversation or chat we often use phrases like, 'Cheer up!' or 'Don't worry', or 'Oh, I don't think you really want to do that'. All of these (and probably you can think of many more) are, in a sense, non-accepting that a person **is** miserable, or anxious or (even if temporarily) does want to do something which we don't see as a good idea. None of this may matter in the normal to-and-fro of conversation, but if we are working empathically, and listening for the other person's point of view, we will have heard that the feelings expressed are real for them now. Full acceptance means acknowledging that reality without needing to criticise, judge or argue with what is being shared.

Acceptance is often seen as one of the most difficult of qualities to develop in ourselves: it means suspending our own values, something none of us finds easy.

Check how accepting you could be of the people who made the following statements. (Remember you aren't required to approve of them, but to respect the person's feelings as real for them.)

> ~ *All politician's are liars or corrupt. Why bother to vote?*
> ~ *There's no point in trying. Nothing ever changes.*
> ~ *Violent criminals should be locked up for life.*
> ~ *Immigrants should be sent back to where they came from.*
> ~ *Religion in schools should be banned.*
> ~ *Mothers should stay home until their children go to school.*
> ~ *People who want to die should be allowed to do so.*
> ~ *Suicide is a mortal sin.*
> ~ *She's going through the grieving process.*
> ~ *There's no justice in this world.*

The ability to avoid the trap of debating the views with which we don't agree is what communicating acceptance is about. We don't have to abandon our views on religion, race, ethics or anything else, but if our intention is to build a trusting relationship with the other person, we have to suspend the judgement and avoid criticism. When we are communicating in palliative care, our aim is to help people trust us, and feel safe enough to explore their situation and themselves as openly and deeply as possible. This may be very painful or frightening for the other person, and would not be helped if they felt criticised. Acceptance is crucial if we want the other person to trust us and to develop a warm relationship with us.

> Compare the two following dialogues for acceptance and then try to formulate a non-accepting and an accepting response to the statements which follow.

1.

Palliative care nurse: I thought I'd better tell you that I've decided to give up; this kind of work isn't really for me.

Line manager: Oh, I don't think you want to do that; there's only a few more months and you'll have your diploma.

Palliative care nurse: Actually, I don't want to work in this field anyway, so the qualification's pointless.

Line manager: Yes, it gets a bit like that with all these assessments coming up. None of us likes exams, do we? But I expect your tutors could give you some help with that.

Palliative care nurse: It's not that. I just don't want to be in nursing any more.

Line manager: I wonder... you're looking a bit strained; how about a few days' leave?

2.

> *Palliative care nurse:* I thought I'd better tell you that I've decided to give up; this kind of work isn't really for me.
>
> *Line manager:* Thank you for coming. You seem really worried.
>
> *Palliative care nurse:* Yes, I'm really in a lot of doubt about whether working in this field is right — for me or for the people I'm caring for.
>
> *Line manager:* You're having doubts about whether palliative care is where you see your future?
>
> *Palliative care nurse:* Yes; I don't know... it all seems so terribly responsible. I don't think I'm up to carrying all of that. It gets too scary.
>
> *Line manager:* Is it maybe that sense of being so responsible for people's last days that gets frightening?

1.

> *Patient:* Why do you keep giving me all these pills? They're not doing me any good and you know it. I think it's just to keep me quiet so that you can have a quiet night or something.

2.

> *Mother of patient in palliative care:* I don't want to be rude my dear, but I just don't think you can understand, in palliative care: you're too young; and only a mother can know what it feels like to lose a son.

3.

> *Husband of very poorly patient:* It's so unfair. The world is full of really evil people that none of us would miss and there's Ellen who never hurt a soul and did everything for everyone else. Why does she have to suffer and not them?

4.

> *Patient:* I've got to start this new treatment tomorrow. I'm terrified. What if they find I'm worse... and what if it doesn't do any good. I don't know... I think it would be better, really, just to give up and let things take their course.

You might have noticed that your non-accepting responses were of a reassuring nature? 'I'm sure you'll be all right' is often a response when we don't quite know how to be realistic, or when we are embarrassed, yet it can be extremely irritating. 'Nothing is more maddening,' said a patient to me, 'than to be told "don't worry", when you're worried to death!' Non-acceptance can also be communicated by trying to debate or dispute issues. In statement 3, for example, there is no answer to the issue of why bad things happen to good people, and not to those seen as 'bad'. We may have beliefs about the problem, or be able to acknowledge that 'there is no justice in the world', or see the issue as so metaphysical that it's not worth contemplating. Trying to convince someone who is troubled by what they see as injustice is unaccepting. It also distracts us into discussion rather than relationship building. 'Yes... but' is often a good indication of being non-accepting!

At some point in a relationship, it may become appropriate to challenge the other person's negative or self-destructive feelings and thoughts. This does not mean that you are no longer accepting these feelings and thoughts as real and painful. As Carl Rogers put it (1967):

> *It involves an acceptance of and caring for the client as a separate person, with permission for him to have his own feelings and experiences and to find his own meanings in them.*

Genuineness/sincerity

The third core quality is very difficult to define precisely or accurately. We **know** when someone is being sincere, but quite **how** we know is not clear. The word has its origins in Roman dishonest trading. Perfect marble has no fissures, but it was comparatively easy to disguise hairline cracks in inferior marble with wax, cerus. Traders who wished to declare the genuineness of their marble, advertised it as 'sine (without) cerus', without wax. A modern equivalent might be something like, 'What you see is what you get.' The idea is very prevalent in the English language; 'the real thing', 'the genuine article', etc. Interestingly, if we look at the other two core qualities we could discuss **how to** understand another's point of view; or **how to** become more accepting. But we can't **how to** 'sincere' – we can only **be** it. Sincerity is a quality which is critical in the relationship-building which is so vital in palliative care.

Think for a moment of times when you feel that you are most yourself. With whom are you most genuine? Where and when do you feel safe enough to disclose the 'real me'? How often do you express what you really feel?

It hardly needs saying that communication is a two-way process but, just as we know when someone is not genuine, so others can spot it in us, and this affects trust. There is a fairly common saying, 'You have to earn people's trust'. What does that saying mean for you?

I think perhaps it contains a paradox. We need to be confident that we are genuinely trustworthy, and in that sense should not have to 'earn' someone's trust. On the other hand, people may need time to learn that we are trustworthy and their experience of trusting people will be very varied. Some of us have had good experiences, but some have felt suspicious or even betrayed and will find trusting very difficult.

> Reflect on your own experiences of trusting and how they have affected your outlook on trusting people.

There is a particular difficulty associated with trust and communicating with people receiving palliative care. Despite a greater openness about the nature of terminal illness, there are still many levels of secrecy. As long ago as 1965 Glaser and Strauss defined four levels of 'awareness' from their observation of dying people, and their communication patterns with those around them. These four contexts of awareness are: (as you look at each brief description, try to think through any issues of trust which there might be.)

Closed awareness

The dying person is 'in the dark' about the terminal nature of their illness; carers and others collude in keeping a veil of secrecy over the issue. Sometimes there is an element of pride about concealing the truth. It is a rather paradoxical state — not least in its name: can one be both 'in the dark' and aware? We might also assume that receiving palliative care might, in itself, mean a degree of openness, but this does not invariably happen.

Suspected awareness

The dying person suspects that their prognosis is poor and this may be confirmed or denied by the behaviours of those around him or her, especially if the behaviour has changed. 'I knew things were bad when they all started being cheerful around me', said one patient. The physical relief brought by a change from curative to palliative care may heighten this level of awareness: the patient may actually feel better and so assume that they will get better. (We might, incidentally, link this with our exploration of hope.) Communication here can be very difficult, especially as far as realism is concerned; trying to establish how aware a patient is, or wants to be, is a delicate task.

Mutual pretence

Glaser and Strauss (1965) consider that at this level both the dying person and those caring for him or her, whether professionals or informal and family carers, are fully in the know about the prognosis, but enter into a sort of conspiracy not to acknowledge the terminal prognosis. There is probably a wide range of reasons for mutual pretence: 'it's too upsetting'; 's/he'll give up the fight'; 'I don't want to depress everyone by talking about it'. Professionals often feel they enter into this 'conspiracy' unwillingly, because it is what the patient and his or her family want. Some professionals, however, express a sense of relief that they are spared what can be a difficult communication area. As we discussed earlier, distancing may be a defence for some of us, and mutual pretence offers opportunity for the safety of distance.

Open awareness

At this level, all parties are able to discuss openly a full range of aspects of the diagnosis. For many palliative care workers, this is seen as the ideal, both for themselves and for those they are helping. It allows discussion of treatment options, practical plans for a will or a funeral, the possibility of spiritual comfort. Conversely, although it may seem ideal, it can be challenging and draining. Open awareness may bring with it fears, ranging from fear of pain, fear of the unknown, of the hereafter, and fear for and of the about-to-be-bereaved. Working with fear is not a job for the faint hearted!

> At which level would you find it easiest to be genuine? Why?

It is difficult to be wholly genuine and sincere when there are secrets of one sort or another, but because complete transparency is so challenging it may feel easier to work at a more superficial level (often disguised under cheeriness). The penalty is that trust may be difficult to establish, or be lost if the patient, or significant others, move to awareness and realise that we have not been genuine. Sincerity and trust are very closely linked.

These three qualities of **empathy**, **acceptance** and **sincerity** are essential if communication is to be received as helpful. You might like to make a list of other desirable qualities; perhaps starting with a well-developed sense of humour.

Learning to develop these qualities in ourselves will enhance the counselling skills (see *Chapters 5* and *6*). Indeed, the skills are not likely to be effective without the qualities, so it is worth expending time and energy on the self-development needed to move towards 'communicating with the whole person'.

On counselling and counselling skills training courses, emphasis is placed on developing self-awareness. The rationale for this is that if we have little self-understanding it will be difficult, if not impossible, to understand others, and if we are unaware of the impact our behaviours have on others, it will be difficult to develop meaningful communication or rewarding relationships. Developing self-awareness requires a high degree of honesty and can sometimes be a rather painful business, but is necessary for helpers and carers, especially in the exceptionally sensitive area of palliative care.

A popular way of considering how we may become more self-aware is the Johari Window (Pfeiffer and Jones, 1972).

Johari Window

How do we become more aware?

	Known to self	Unknown	
Known to others	Open	Feed back	Blind
	Self disclosure	INSIGHT	
Unknown to others	Hidden		"Unknown"

1. 'Open' area   to self and others, 'on top of table.'
2. 'Blind' area   unknown to self but apparent to others.
3. 'Hidden' area   known to self, hidden to others, 'under the table,'
4. 'Unknown' area   to self and to others, potential available but not yet discovered.

The free or open area is our 'public' face: the person we are quite happy to let others see and interact with. This is the area which we need to enlarge if we are to become more self-aware.

The 'blind' area may include non-verbal mannerisms, tone of voice, attitudes and really good personality traits of which you are unaware. Receiving feedback, which is responsibly given, can help you discover what really helps or hinders your communication with others. If the feedback is supportive, it can enlarge our understanding of how others may perceive us and facilitate the developing or deepening of relationships.

The 'hidden' area is the self that we know well, but are very wary about sharing with others. To open up this area requires trust that the other person, or persons, will not abuse any self-disclosure that we might make.

The final area contains the unrecognised strengths, abilities and creativity which we ourselves have never explored and therefore others have never seen. The area can also, of course, contain darker elements of our personality and especially our fears. This is especially relevant to work in palliative care, where the more imminent prospect of death may reveal previously buried fears associated with mortality (our own and others').

The theory is that the more we can widen the 'open' or 'free' area of ourselves, the fewer tensions we will experience and the more we will be able to communicate our true selves. The reward is that those for whom we are caring will be helped to communicate their true selves to us.

> Go through each 'pane' of the Johari window and reflect on how you could create opportunities for enlarging the free or open area of yourself. Try to relate each opportunity to palliative care. Remember, though, that generally speaking, self-disclosure often feels risky; feed-back frequently provokes defensiveness; insight may be explosive.

Another method of developing self-awareness is to see ourselves through three processes:

1. Description

2. Explanation
3. Prediction

1. It is useful to think of as many ways as possible to describe ourselves – physically, emotionally, socially, intellectually. A good way of doing this is to think in terms of metaphors and similes – I'm like a child on its birthday; I'm a juggler who's afraid the plates will fall. We can share our lists with others and this will help us with self-disclosure, and with hearing whether others agree or disagree with our self-image. Incidentally, sensitive use of imagery can also help with communicating empathically.
2. If we draw a time line of our lives and mark on it significant events, we can work at trying to explain why we made the choices we did and how these led to or affected the next significant event. You might also draw a time line which marks events and choices which led to your interest in palliative care.

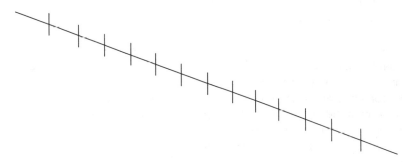

3. Predicting how we will react to given experiences can hardly be an exact science! If it were, we would probably be little more than programmed robots. On the other hand, we frequently say things like, 'I know just what will happen: I'll... I always do'. We also like to think that we can predict how others will react. Sometimes the converse is true and we are surprised at how wrong our predictions can be: 'If you'd asked me before, I never would have thought that I'd...'.

Being able to predict at least some of our reactions can help with genuineness. If we can think ahead to situations where we might feel embarrassed or uncomfortable we are less likely to be surprised or defensive if and when they occur. This is especially important in palliative care where situations are often demanding.

> Look at the following list, or make one of your own, and try to pre-
> dict how you would react. Write down your responses so that if
> similar situations arise you can check your predictions about your
> thoughts and feelings.
>
> A patient seems unable to stop crying
>
> A patient begins to give you explicit details about his sex
> life
>
> You find another carer is racist
>
> A patient's relative is verbally abusive and uses obscene
> language
>
> You are asked questions about your religious beliefs in a **very**
> demanding way
>
> A patient tells you s/he has fallen in love with you
>
> (all these are real situations confronted by home care nurses from
> various hospices.)
>
> Could you communicate holistically with the speakers?

If we are aiming for holistic care and to communicate with the whole
person using counselling skills effectively, we need to develop the core
qualities and to increase self-awareness. As a final exercise in preparation
for using counselling skills, look at the following diagram of the process
of communication. The whole process may take only a fraction of time,
or it might be quite lengthy. It's important to see ourselves as both the
giver (transmitter) and as the receiver. We need an awareness of where in
the cycle patients may be when they are trying to communicate with us
and what we are doing when we try to communicate with them.

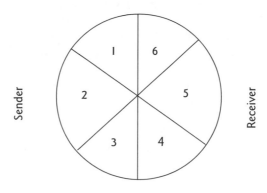

1. A message is conceived. We make a decision to communicate as a result of an impulse, which might be external or internal (a thought or feeling), to which we respond.
2. The message is 'encoded'. We select the 'language' in which to transmit the message. It may be oral, written word, a picture or some form of non-verbal communication.
3. The 'medium' for the message is chosen, eg. if we are writing we might choose a letter or memo or e-mail. If oral, we could telephone or talk one-to-one with the other person. Non-verbally, we might use touch.
4. The message is 'decoded'. The receiver will read or hear the message within their own knowledge and understanding of the terms used (eg. specialised vocabulary) or the context.
5. The message is interpreted. The receiver will interpret both any underlying meaning as well as the more explicit meaning. There might be serious distortion.
6. Feedback is given (or withheld). Signals are passed back to the sender in a variety of forms.

As you can see, the process may be continuous, but there are a variety of points at which it might break down.

> Take two examples from your palliative care experience. One when you were the transmitter, and one when you were the receiver. Reflect on how the process worked in each situation and whether it could have been improved.

To consolidate your understanding of this chapter, try to answer the following questions:

1. What do you think is the difference between palliative care and palliative medicine? In what ways do you think the two do or should complement each other?
2. What are the limitations on holistic communication?
3. How essential to holistic communication do you think the three core qualities are?
4. Why is self-awareness seen as crucial for effective palliative care? Do you agree that it is an essential factor? Why/why not? Could self-awareness inhibit spontaneity?
5. 'Without theory and underpinning understanding, counselling skills are empty techniques'. What is your view of this statement?

References

Egan G (1992) *The Skilled Helper.* 4th edn. Monterey Books, Cole
Glaser BG, Strauss AL (1965) *Awareness of Dying.* Aldine, Chicago
Griffin J (1991) *Dying with Dignity.* Office of Health Economics, London
National Council for Hospice and Specialist Palliative Care Services (1992)
Pfeiffer, Jones (1972) *Structured Experiences for Human Relations Training.*
    University Associates, California
Rogers C (1967) *On Becoming A Person.* Constable, London
Rogers C (1980) *A Way Of Being.* Houghton Mifflin, Boston
Walter TA (1996) A new model for grief: bereavement and biography. *Mortality*
    1: 7–25

5

Counselling skills

What are counselling skills?

The British Association for Counselling and Psychotherapy (BACP) offers this definition (1997):

> *Counselling skills are being used when:*
> *There is an intentional use of specific interpersonal skills, which reflects the values of counselling, and the user's primary role (eg. nurse, tutor, line manager, social worker, personnel officer, helper) is enhanced without them taking on the role of counsellor, and:*
> *The recipient perceives the user as acting within their primary professional/caring rôle, which is not that of a counsellor.*

Several points emerge from this definition:

❀ Counselling skills are specific — that is, we can identify and name them.
❀ They should be used with 'intention', which seems to mean that we should know what we are doing when we use the skills and should not be using them in a haphazard way.
❀ The skills are interpersonal; using them involves active interaction with another.
❀ The skills are underpinned by values. We need to be clear about the values of counselling if we are to reflect them, even though we may not be counsellors or be counselling.
❀ Counselling skills enhance the primary role. In our case, the role of palliative carer is improved and heightened (or even, in the terms of one dictionary, 'made more beautiful' by the use of the skills).

❦ Counselling and counselling skills are different, and the recipient should see us in our palliative care role and not as a counsellor (although, of course, many palliative care teams do include counsellors).

> Look through each of these points before we examine some of them in greater detail and jot down any queries you may have, or any points which you find contentious.

Values

The values of counselling, which the skills should 'reflect', are contained within those three core conditions of **empathy**, **respect** and **sincerity**. The BACP code (1997) says:

> *The practitioner using counselling skills will respect*
> *the client's values, experience, thoughts, feelings,*
> *and their capacity for self-determination, and aims*
> *to serve the best interests of the client.*

There is an underlying assumption here that we will have established what a client's values are in order to be able to respect them. As we have seen, in palliative care this is not easy, as values about dying and death may vary enormously from patient to patient and from carer to carer. In terms of self-awareness, we also need to be clear what our own value system is, especially as some values may be culturally acquired and could be different from those acquired in another culture.

> Brain-storm a list of what you see as your personal value system. If possible, compare your list with another person's.

A well-known writer on interpersonal and counselling skills, Richard Nelson-Jones (1996), suggests that the following list of values are those which we (consciously or unconsciously) bring to relationships. You can probably see that many items could be assumed from Maslow's hierarchy. Compare Nelson-Jones' list with yours, remembering that we are thinking about what we value, rather than what we need or want:

- love
- friendship and social responsibility

- survival
- family life
- security
- faith/belief/religion
- success and a career
- materialism ('owning', eg. property, possessions)
- aesthetics (approving beauty in, for example. music, art, home)
- intelligence
- excitement
- conformity ('fitting in') and tradition
- having fun
- practical (valuing being able to 'do something')
- nature
- health
- independence.

> Try to rate each of our values:
>   a) in terms of your own personal growth and development
> and b) in terms of what you bring to relationships in palliative
>   care.

Counselling skills, the code tells us, are 'interpersonal'. In *Nurse–Client Interaction* (1976), Sundeen states that:

> *Quality... care is dependent on the therapeutic use
> of self.*

To be effective however, the carer needs to be sensitive to what is happening on both sides of the interaction. It is not much use thinking that we have and are deepening and developing the core conditions or that we are clear about our own and respectful of others' values, if the other person does not perceive this. It is by 'intentional use of specific... skills' that we communicate our help and support. It is the skills which enable the **therapeutic** use of self.

Think of an exchange, personal, social or professional, which you wish you had handled differently. Then try to answer to following questions:

- did you realise beforehand that the interaction might be difficult?
- where did you approach the other person?
- how did you approach him/her?
- what facial or other non-verbal expressions did you use? How do you know?
- what did you say?
- how did you say it?
- what made the encounter difficult?
- how did you feel immediately afterwards?
- now?
- what might you do differently if you had the chance?

Now, go through the list again seeing yourself as a palliative care patient or relative who wants to ask some sensitive questions or questions which require courage to broach. How would they perceive you?

If you look through the questions, you will perhaps see that the essential skills probably fall into four categories. Firstly, we will have been trying to gauge or sum-up the other person, perhaps to work out their mood, by **observing** them. Then, from the setting and the way in which we approached the person, there must be a sense of **attentiveness** — the other person will realise that we are giving them our full attention.

We will have **listened** to them: not only to what they were saying, but also to how they were feeling, and then **responded** in a way which sensitively showed that we had heard both content and feeling. The 'specific interpersonal skills' advocated by BACP fall into these four categories, and if you can recall a time when you felt someone had really heard something important which you wanted to convey, you will probably find that the person had a range of skills within each category. These first level counselling skills are usually placed under the heading of **active listening**.

What, for you, is the difference between listening and active listening?

Perhaps at the heart of the difference is that when I am listening, the other person or persons, need not, necessarily, know that I am listening. An extreme example of this would be listening to music on a radio, where the performer (or person playing the recording) can have no knowledge of how intently I may be listening. **Active** listening means demonstrating that I hear, that I'm trying to understand, that I am engaged; it is a dynamic process, whereas listening can be a passive process. When we listen actively we are not only showing the other person that we are listening, we are also encouraging the talker to express their thoughts, feelings and concerns, prompting them if they get stuck or find continuing difficult. Active listening means being both physically and psychologically 'with' the other person. It creates warmth and is the foundation of relationship building. Meaningful communication takes place in the context of a warm and trusting relationship. The four skills areas of attention giving, observing, listening and responding constitute active listening.

Attention giving

In the list of questions which you answered about a difficult encounter, you will have noticed that there is an underlying sense that it is helpful to be prepared. We can demonstrate that we are paying attention by preparing both ourselves and the setting, and this is especially important in palliative care, where we are communicating in a particularly sensitive arena.

> How do you prepare yourself for communicating with a patient or relative?

Getting ourselves ready to listen actively to a patient or to relatives can involve being sure that we have the time. If we are worried that we have other things to do, or that we really should be somewhere else, it is unlikely that we shall listen, much less listen actively. Patients will pick up that we are 'on pins' and the interaction is unlikely to be therapeutic. It would probably show more respect to explain that you want to give your full attention and will do so at a given time. We can also prepare ourselves by practising putting our own worries and concerns 'on the back burner'. This is not as easy as it sounds, but it is worthwhile making that effort, because there is evidence that not doing so seriously affects empathy. We can also make a conscious decision to set aside our own value system for the duration of the time we spend with the other person. It is important to have the humility to accept that our beliefs and values may, for the patient, be wholly irrelevant. I may believe strongly that assisted suicide is wrong, but it will not enable a patient to talk about his views that, 'you wouldn't let a pet go through this', if I am not prepared to set aside my views and encourage him to share his. Personal preparation can also be helped by self-awareness: we need to think carefully about how others see us.

> Stand in front of a full-length mirror and try to gauge how you would be seen by:
> - a relative of a dying child
> - a dying child
> - a patient in remission
> - an HIV/AIDS patient
> - an 'at home' patient in a poor environment
> - an angry patient 'in denial'.

The way we look conveys a great deal to others — whether this is 'fair' is a moot point. When we are working interpersonally, we need to be able to convey sincerity and that means being natural, being one's self, and anxiety about how the other person perceives us (especially at a first meeting) can impede this. There is a difference between being self-conscious and being self-aware; learning how to walk the line between the two is part of good preparation. Attentiveness can also be shown by good preparation of the setting. Research shows that settings can have an enormous impact on the quality of an interaction.

Look at this statement given by a hospice volunteer:

> *I was amazed. I'd always talked to him at St...'s and we had the quiet room to ourselves. Looking back, I can see that I probably felt safe (in all sorts of ways) there and I certainly didn't react when he made comments like, 'Posh here, isn't it?' Then he got too poorly to come and I visited him at home. 'Home' turned out to be on a somewhat dubious estate, with a lot of boarded up houses. The television was on non-stop; relatives wandered in and out and their cat wanted to sit on me... to be honest, I can't remember much of what we covered that day.*

This demonstrates how profoundly setting can influence active listening. (It also highlights how setting affects the balance of power in an interaction.) Just as we aim to minimise distractions in ourselves, we can try to minimise distractions in the setting. Trying to ensure that there are no interruptions; turning off 'bleeps' or mobile phones are obvious examples. Obviously we cannot always have the luxury of our volunteer's 'quiet room', but by giving some thought to making the best of the setting where we are working, we can demonstrate our preparedness and willingness to listen.

> Make a check list of how you could maximise the environment in which you talk to people involved in palliative care:
> 1. Seating (especially if the patient is in bed)
> 2.
> 3.
> 4.

Active listening involves listening with the whole self: our non-verbal as well as our verbal communication.

Here are some figures from research (Bayliss, 1970). In communication:

7%	is	content (what we say)
38%	is	tone (how we say it)
55%	is	non-verbal

Does this surprise you? Perhaps even more surprising is the research finding that when verbal and non-verbal messages conflict, we tend to 'hear' and believe the non-verbal message (I expect you can see how this relates to the core condition of genuineness/sincerity). Non-verbal communication seems to be especially influential in first encounters and will affect the subsequent quality of a relationship in a variety of ways.

> Listen to a sports commentary (especially the commentary of a tennis match) and notice the references to the contestants' body language. (Sometimes you might find the interpretations rather fanciful.)

This aspect of active listening is frequently represented by an acronym, which may be familiar to you:

$$S - O - L - E - R$$

S **Setting** (maximising the environment)
  Seating (be aware of distance, height, obstacles).

O **Open** posture (get your own seating right). We need to be comfortable so that we won't be fidgeting and so that folded arms, for instance, don't give the impression that we are defensive (or just cold).

L **Lean**. If we lean too far forward could this be threatening? If we lean too far back, would this be perceived as too casual? What might rigid uprightness convey?

E **Eye contact**. This can be a very difficult area to feel natural with — staring is threatening, frequent looking away can be distracting. There are also cultural issues to be considered. In the West there is a tendency to see direct eye contact as a sign of honesty. If someone won't or can't make eye contact, there is a tendency to think that they may have something to hide. Indeed they may well, but this may say much more about our ability to convey trustworthiness than about the person's honesty. Parents and teachers quite frequently use eye-contact as part of discipline: 'Look at me when I'm talking to you!' — and a legacy like this may be hard to shake off. It may, for many patients, be easier to broach difficult topics **without** eye contact.

R **Relax**. Check for signs of tension. Tense non-verbals are almost contagious and will not help the patient.

One aspect of non-verbal communication which needs careful and honest consideration is touch. What can be more natural, when we sense or see that someone is upset or hurt, than to give a comforting clasp of the hand, or to put an arm around the person? Yet we need to be very careful about whether we are meeting our own needs to comfort via touch, or the person's need. How do we **know** that the person wants or needs to be touched?

Checking through all of these will help us to demonstrate the attention-giving component of active listening.

Observing and noticing

Just as patients and their relatives perceive many things from our non-verbal communication and make assumptions about how fully we are paying attention, in the same way can we learn from careful observation of their non-verbal communication. There is a wealth of information for us to respond to if we are sensitive to what we see, as well as to what we hear. Paradoxical though it may seem, active listening involves listening with our eyes as well as with our ears, in order to understand everything that patients and relatives offer us.

A useful exercise can be to watch a piece of film with no sound and to interpret the facial expressions and gestures of the actors or people. Then rewind the film and replay with the sound and check whether our interpretations were accurate.

Since we all have prejudices and biases, these can sometimes get in the way of accurate observation. Once again, self-awareness is critical: if we do not know our own prejudices we will not be able to check whether they are 'filtering' our observation.

> Watch a group of people, perhaps on a train or bus, or on television if this is your only opportunity. Notice your reactions to each person. For example, if there is a shaven headed male, with tattoos and wearing a singlet, with a gap between it and his jeans, what are your assumptions?

Putting aside assumptions is part of unconditional positive regard, of course, but few if any of us have no prejudices; the crucial point is to be aware of them so that they do not interfere with our observation of non-verbal cues or clues. Active listening means, in part, observing accurately.

There are two aspects to observation skills. Firstly, we can **draw an inference**. Sometimes the non-verbal cues can seem to contradict the words which are being said and sometimes they can seem to be at odds with each other. We can sometimes help others to explore issues by drawing an inference from such contradictions.

> *You say that you really don't miss having people drop round, yet at the same time you seem to be swallowing back your feelings. Would it be helpful to look at how these two match up for you?*

> *I notice that when you talk about your illness, you clench your jaw and fists like someone who's very angry, but at the same time your eyes are tearful. Could we explore this perhaps...?*

> Try for a week to monitor your observations, the inferences you drew from them and whether or not you responded accurately.

Any inferences that we draw need to be very tentative — the patient may look tearful because s/he is suppressing a yawn!

The second component of observation skills is the ability to pick up on **behavioural cues or clues**. Behavioural cues are habits which people seem to have as a way of expressing feelings.

> Try to think what you **do** when you are:
>
> angry
> sad
> frustrated
> bored
> trying to avoid doing something
> thwarted.

Noticing how clients express their feelings, particularly if there is a pattern, is an important part of active listening. Even if we choose not to respond, we are storing up a wealth of information about patients and relatives which will enhance our relationship-building and understanding.

A word of warning, others will be observing our cues and clues and 'reading' us too. 'When you frown like that you remind me of my mother', for example, may be a response when we were unaware of the frown and if it had 'meaning' it was that we were concentrating. Clearly it means something for the other person, and that something may be very significant.

Listening

This is probably one of the most over-used words in connection with counselling and counselling skills. It is, of course, the most valuable of all the skills, but its complexity is not always realised. Trainers hear, 'I'm a good listener,' offered very frequently by would-be trainees in counselling or counselling skills, but probing what this actually means does not always produce very precise definitions.

> What, for you, makes a 'good listener'?
> What makes **you** a 'good listener'?

Genuinely 'good listeners' seem to be able to do several things at once. They can:

- take in accurately the content which is being conveyed, and often recall it in the right order
- hear the feelings which accompany each part of the content
- listen to the whole message without feeling the need to interrupt
- tolerate silence, and 'hear' what it might mean.

Good listening then is a complex activity and requires sustained effort.

> Ask a friend to talk to you for about five minutes about something which matters to them. Write down, or repeat what was said, if possible in order. How accurate were you? (This exercise can be usefully practised on audio tape.)

If we only hear content we are only half listening to what is being said; or listening to only half of what is said. Listening actively to feelings requires us to be alert to how patients or their relatives are feeling **now** (rather than how they may describe how they **felt** about an incident or person).

Think about this scenario, given by a palliative care nurse in clinical supervision:

> *Her patient was really upset. He had lost patience*
> *with his wife (his primary carer) because he felt she*
> *was robbing him of what little independence he had*
> *left. He described how he had hurled his lunch tray*
> *on the floor, and said that he didn't want 'pap', and*
> *shouted at her to leave him alone to die in peace.*

The nurse's task here was to listen to how the patient feels now, and to try to establish what 'upset' (a rather vague word) might mean. She cannot do this by listening, however accurately, only to the content. She needs to hear how the patient feels now if she is to respond sensitively. She will need to notice whether he still seems angry, or if he is regretful. If he sounded gleeful, she might have to suspend any value judgements about the behaviour. The question, 'how do you feel about that?' has become such a cliché that it has virtually become a joke in counselling. Good listeners will see it as their responsibility to determine how others feel by listening to how they **sound**. There are reckoned to be ten main barriers to good listening.

> Make a list of the barriers you perceive and then check them against the given list.

Barriers to good listening

'Off-'n'-on'

Most of us think about four times as quickly as an average speaker. As listeners we have three quarters of 'spare' time for every minute we listen. It is all too easy to use the time to think about our own affairs.

Open ears, but closed mind

We start off listening, especially to content, but quickly decide that we know what is coming next and switch off because what will be said we have predicted and, perhaps, find it boring.

'Red rag'

The expression 'red rag to a bull' can apply to listening. Some words are flash points and make us irritated or angry and we stop listening. Some examples are, 'must'; 'should/ought'; the health service; Government. Death and dying are also potent triggers for some people.

'I can't cope with this'

Sometimes what is being shared seems too complex and complicated, so we stop trying. Patients often complain that the language professionals use about illness is so technical: 'I'm no wiser than I was before'.

Drift

We have good intentions and look intensely interested but, especially if we're tired, we drift off, become glassy eyed and develop a rather dreamy expression. We can tell when others do this to us, and similarly, others know when we are the culprits.

Problem not person listening

Many problems, especially in palliative care do not have a 'solution'. Listening to the problem rather than to how the person feels about the problem can be a barrier.

Clash

We have our own pet ideas, prejudices and points of view. When a speaker says something which clashes with these we stop listening and instead plan how we will correct the speaker, or will argue and debate the point made.

Noise

External and internal distractions affect good listening.

Note taking

If we try to take down everything said we shall miss much; eye contact becomes difficult and feelings get lost.

Memory

We may become so conscious of trying to remember everything shared that we mentally repeat each point and then get lost as the speaker has moved on.

> Try to award yourself marks out of ten next week for every pitfall you avoid.

In palliative care work there may be additional barriers created by the dying person and his or her relatives and friends. These may range from difficulty in expressing thoughts and feelings about the illness or about mortality, to physical barriers created by the illness or by medication.

You will have noticed that the three skill areas we have looked at: namely, attend, observe, listen are all silent skills. This probably represents the balance as it should be in helping interviews — only one quarter should need to be spoken by the listener. Counselling skills are about 'You talk, I listen' rather than the other way around. The fourth skill cluster, **respond**, also indicates that the helping interview should be led by the talker, we respond to what is shared rather than trying to lead and to find out what we want to know. This makes the interview rather different from the medical model, where the objective is to find out what we want to know. It is worth noting in this context that one dictionary definition of respond is 'to show sensitiveness towards'.

There seem to be four responding skills which every user of counselling skills needs to have in their 'tool kit'.

> **What do you think they are?**
> 1.
> 2.
> 3.
> 4.

The four basic skills are usually thought to be:

- asking questions
- paraphrasing
- reflecting
- summarising.

Questions

It is sometimes suggested that questions are a way of controlling an interaction.

> **What is your opinion of this view?**

The thinking is that questions tend to come from the listener's frame of reference and that they move the focus from:

> *You talk, I listen.*

to

> *I talk; you listen.*

The power tends to lie with the questioner. Sometimes, questions interrupt a flow of feeling or a train of thought, which may cause the speaker to dry up, or they may answer but then go back to their original concern. The problem could be that the relationship becomes de-railed and may take valuable time to get back on track.

Look at these questions, given in response to genuine patient or relative statements, and try to decide if they are helpful or unhelpful to the speaker.

1.

> *Very frail patient:* Just for once, I had a really happy weekend. We managed to go out and I even had a pint!
> *Listener:* What are your plans for next weekend?

2.

> *Relative:* I know it's silly, but when his breathing gets difficult I start to panic and get into a real sweat, even though I know it will pass.
> *Listener:* Would you like a leaflet about dyspnoea?

3.

> *Colleague on palliative care team:* Every time I hear her voice I cringe. I just hate the way she operates.
> *Listener:* Have you asked to work on a different team?

4.

> *Relative:* So I told him we **did not want** the treatment and I didn't care what he did so long as he left us alone.
> *Listener:* Who are you talking about?

In general, there are four types of question:

1. Open
2. Closed
3. Multiple
4. Leading

Closed questions

These can be useful when we need to determine factual points, but as a counselling skill they are, on the whole, better avoided as they tend to close down rather than open up areas for discussion, particularly if the answer is just 'yes' or 'no'. They also mean that the control of the discussion is very firmly with the questioner.

Open questions

These, on the other hand, leave the choice of what to share with the speaker and can encourage good exploration, especially in the early stages of relationship-building. Open questions usually start with; how? what? where? and help us to avoid the trap of closed questions where the yes/no answer means that we have to ask yet another question... and another... and the person begins to feel interrogated.

> Try turning these closed questions into open questions:
>
> Have you told your wife?
> Do you want to talk to me?
> Are you always tearful about this?
> Does this upset you?
> Have you been feeling like this for long?
> Are you in pain?

Multiple questions

These are best avoided for various reasons. Firstly, several questions in one sentence can confuse since it is difficult to be sure which one to answer:

> *Is it that you're feeling low today or has someone*
> *upset you or perhaps it's your medication?*

It would take a brave patient to say 'Er, which shall I answer first?'

Secondly, we restrict the speaker's choice of answer — the options we choose to offer may not be relevant to him or her.

Thirdly, by providing the answers ourselves we are forgetting that core quality of respect.

Questioning successfully means helping the other person to clarify and asking several questions in one does just the opposite.

Egan, whose model of helping is probably the best known, says:

> *If a helper asks two questions in a row, one at least*
> *is stupid.*

Strong words, but worth reminding ourselves of.

Leading questions

These are also best avoided.

> Listen to a radio or TV interview and notice the frequency of questions which being with '*Surely*' or '*But surely...*' or begin with a negative, '*Don't you think/agree...*', '*Isn't it the case that...*'. Often, leading questions will end with something like '*... weren't you?*', '*... wasn't s/he/it?*'

This may be appropriate when interviewing a politician who may be avoiding or evading, but is counter-productive when trying to work sensitively with a sick person and his or her relatives or, indeed, with our own colleagues. Here is an example of a well-meaning use of a leading question to a wife who had nursed her rather demanding husband to the end and was asked, 'I'm sure you were devastated when the end came, weren't you, even though you were expecting it?' The wife told me, 'Actually I felt nothing but relief, but I didn't have the courage to correct him.'

Leading questions are based on an assumption that we know how the other person thinks or feels and that it will be as we think or feel. This is hardly respectful.

> Test your responses to these leading questions:
> Surely you don't agree with assisted suicide?
> Aren't you glad he died at home/in hospital/at the hospice?
> Don't you think you should tell them?

A word about **why?** Sometimes why? questions can be helpful and it is 'open', but it can block or divert the speaker.

- 'Why do you think your mother/father/etc does that or thinks that?' **may** open up new perspectives, but it can equally move the focus from the talker (where it belongs) to the third person. In a sense, too, it can only be speculation as the only person who can answer the question is the mother/father etc.
- Asking the person themselves why they do this or that implies that they know the answer. Perhaps the very reason they seek help is because they **don't** know and we could be 'putting them on the spot' to come up with an answer they don't have.
- Sometimes knowing the reason 'why' is not part of helping. This is especially so in palliative care, where the reasons for sadness, anger or other emotions are clear and we need to move beyond them.

Look at these questions:

⌘ Why are you so upset?
⌘ Why not just tell them to go away?
⌘ Why do you think s/he's so persistent?
⌘ Why didn't you tell me before?

Here are some 'blind alley' answers to them:

⌘ 'I don't know, I just am.'
⌘ 'I couldn't offend them.'
⌘ 'How would I know?'
⌘ 'I couldn't.'

When you ask questions try to check whether they really help the talker.

Paraphrase and reflection

> Remind yourself of the two levels of listening

We can listen for the facts, for information, but we can also (and more deeply) listen for feelings. Paraphrase and reflection involve a sort of playing back to the speaker what we have heard. **Paraphrase** lets the speaker know that we heard the facts accurately; **reflection** demonstrates that we are also empathising with feeling(s).

It is unfortunate (and rather unfair) that paraphrase has got confused with sounding like some kind of 'echo', when the last few words of a sentence are repeated:

> *I feel sad*   *My life is wretched*
> *You feel sad ...*   *Your life is wretched ...*

This sort of thing could infuriate, but it is nevertheless important to keep alongside the person so that they know we are listening and so that we can check out our accuracy. This need not turn us into parrots. Re-phrasing what was said can be very helpful in giving back to the speaker the 'gist' of what was said without adding or taking away anything significant.

> Try to develop your vocabulary so that you can play back, in **your** words, what was said. Here are some statements to practise with. Remember that you are just rephrasing content:
>
> *Volunteer:* Sometimes the patients get me down. Whatever you do, it's not right or not enough.
>
> *Patient:* It's all right for you young things. Wait till you're my age — things look different them.
>
> *Relative:* I can't stand it really — I'm no nurse and she's so demanding.
>
> *Colleague:* I sit in these meetings and nothing ever changes. We'd be better off working with the patients.

In terms of self-awareness and barriers to good listening it is important not to get so caught up in hunting for synonyms that we forget to listen. Suspending value judgement so that we paraphrase accurately is not always easy.

Reflection, as the word implies, is a sort of mirror, showing the speaker that we are not only listening to facts but have heard **and accepted** that the feelings behind the facts are real for him or her.

> Get a friend to read a variety of short statements to you and try to hear what feeling is being conveyed, then paraphrase the statement and reflect the feeling. Here is an example of a Macmillan nurse using paraphrase and reflection with a patient:
>
> John, when you were describing how difficult you find it to talk to your children about the future (**paraphrase**), you sounded quite angry and frustrated (**reflection**) as if you want to communicate something but feel a bit blocked.

Reflection is a demonstration of **respect** ('I can hear that your feelings are real for you') and **empathy** ('I'm trying to understand how things are for you').

A difficult responding skill to manage and develop is being able to **respond to silence**. There are many types of silence, some comfortable, some not so comfortable. We need to learn our own 'silence threshold' – the ability to tolerate silence and be able to intervene appropriately. There are two main obstacles to responding to silence. We can jump in too soon, because we feel uncomfortable, interrupting some useful thinking or inner struggle that may be going on. Conversely, we can just 'sit it out' until the person 'gives in' and says something, anything. Too often, silence becomes a sort of competition as to who can sit it out longest. Obviously this is not helpful.

Responding to silence as a counselling skill, involves good use of our observation skills and watching carefully for non-verbal signals: does the person look at you expectantly? Are they clearly deep in thought? Sometimes a response to silence, especially if tears are present, prompts the use of touch and again we need to remind ourselves of its acceptability.

> Practise ways of intervening in a silence. For example:
> 'Meg, you seem lost in thought; would it be helpful to share what's going on for you just now?'

The last of the basic responding counselling skills is summarising. At various points in an interview it can help to summarise, it can give the work more structure and help to keep focus, especially if there is a great deal of material, or if the person is rather rambling and seems to find getting to the point rather difficult. Egan (1999) has a few stern words to say about summarising too:

> *A summary is not a mechanical pulling together of a number of facts.*

If all we can summarise is the facts, we have only been half listening, summary is more than ticking off what we have heard.

> See if you can summarise the following scenario using condensed paraphrase and reflection, taking nothing away and adding nothing:
>
> > The problem goes on and on. I really want to tell them that it isn't that I don't want them here, but that sometimes I'm exhausted or in pain and just *can't* put a brave face on. Then I get all guilty because they've made an effort to see me and I'm miserable as sin. Also some of my problems are very embarrassing and it's not pleasant for either of us. I don't know, I think the sooner I'm gone the better for all of us.

Most counselling skills courses suggest that there are three main ways of summarising and it is worth mastering these even if you have your own natural technique. They are:

- contrast
- choice point
- figure and ground.

Contrast

After sensitive summarising of the material, the client is offered the possibility of working on a contrast. In the previous scenario this might be:

> *... (the summary), it seems as if on the one hand you'd like to be more welcoming to your visitors, but on the other there are times when you wish they'd stay away. Let's look at each in turn.*

Choice point

After the summary, the speaker is reassured that everything they shared seems important, but which point would it help to focus on first. This helps the person to prioritise.

Figure and ground

If you look at the landscape or at a painting, usually something (the figure) will stand out from the (back) ground. Tentative reflection of what seems to you to be the 'figure' can help focus. Being tentative is critical because the client must feel able to reject the suggestion.

> *John, of all the problems you've shared with me, −*
> *− − − − − seemed to stand out. If I'm right, shall we explore that first, and come back to the others?*

It is interesting that offering figure-and-ground can really help the person decide on the priorities and, if their choice is to reject our perception, we can feel pleased that we've done well.

Summary can really help to move an interview forward or on to a deeper level of communication.

These four skills areas are the basic counselling skills which form the foundation of communicating in palliative care. Buckman (1988) offers us a very sound rationale for using these skills:

> *1. Talking to each other happens to be the best method of communication we have.*
>
> *2. Simply talking about distress helps to relieve it ... you don't have to have the answers — just listening to the questions can help.*
>
> *3. Thoughts that a person tries to shut out will do harm eventually... conversations between patients and their relatives and friends do not create new fears and anxieties. In fact, the opposite is true; not talking about a fear makes it bigger. Bottled up feelings may also cause shame. One of the greatest services you can do... is to hear and stay close once you've listened. By not backing away or withdrawing, you then show that you accept and understand fears.*

To complete your learning from this chapter, try to answer the following questions:

1. Try to explain how responding links to the core qualities.
2. What do you understand by the 'power base' in connection with questioning?
3. Can you explain the difference between paraphrase and reflection?
4. List all the ways you can show attention without speaking.
5. Why is summary useful and when would you do it?

References

Bayliss JV (1970) Unpublished

British Association for Counselling and Psychotherapy (1997) *Code of ethics and practice for those using counselling skills in their work.* BACP, Rugby

Buckman R (1988) *I Don't Know What To Say.* Macmillan, London

Egan G (1999) *The Skilled Helper.* Brooks-Cole Publishing Company, California

Nelson-Jones R (1996) *Relating Skills: a practical guide to effective personal relationships.* Cassell, London

Sundeen SJ *et al* (1976) *Nurse – Client Interaction.* C V Mosby, St Louis

6

More advanced counselling skills

Although the basic counselling skills reviewed in *Chapter 5* should always be present, as a helping relationship develops and as trust grows, a more complex range of skills may be needed.

One of the major losses experienced by patients receiving palliative care is their sense of independence. Although we all feel fragile from time to time, and may need someone to lean on, most people like to feel self-determining. As a motor-neurone patient put it:

> *Illness robs you. First of all it robs you physically and you have to get others to do things for you, even really intimate things. Then it robs you intellectually; you start not being able to think for yourself, every decision gets made for you. And in the end you just stop feeling and give up emotionally.*

Since the sense of loss is so holistic and our care aims to be holistic, one of our goals should be to enable as much self-reliance as possible. Holistic care may involve any of the following

Taking action

Doing things for patients and relatives.

Advising

Explaining what would be the best course of action.

Changing a system

Trying to ensure that organisations, institutions do not become an obstacle.

Teaching

Helping to learn new skills (eg. using a syringe driver) or ways of coping.

Informing

Offering value-free, factual information.

Counselling

Working to enable greater self-understanding.

Supporting/befriending

Providing sensitive emotional care.

> Review the care that you give, and try to reflect on what proportion of time you give to each. Would you like to change the balance?

If we visualise the helping strategies as a continuum, or a spectrum, an interesting aspect emerges:

Interventions on the left make the assumption that the helper is in control (and this may, of course, be necessary). As we move around the spectrum towards the right, the patient or relative takes more control. On the left the helper has the answers (or at least some of them); on the right, the patient or relative has the answers. The more advanced counselling skills which we look at in this chapter can enhance all of the interventions, but are especially valuable the further to the right of the continuum or spectrum we move.

> Would you agree that the further along the spectrum/continuum you go, the deeper the relationship is likely to be?
> Try to explain this.

We could make the first three interventions with little involvement by the other person(s) and, again, this may sometimes be necessary, but once we reach 'Teach' this involvement becomes necessary and as we move on, we have to trust them to choose for themselves. For example, if I am advising, I might give someone three pieces of useful information, and add '... and I think the best one for you would be...'. If, on the other hand, I give the information only, I am trusting the other person to decide for themselves what is best for them. This is not to say that information is better than advising (or, indeed, that any of the interventions is 'better' than any other), but it is different and the chief difference lies in allowing the other person more choice and control.

> Find an example from your palliative care experience of each of the helping interventions.
>
> Against each example list the skills which you used.

Clearly the quality of the relationship we have with the other person and the degree to which we feel assured of their self-reliance will affect how we communicate. Those basic counselling skills of attend, observe, listen and respond will be invaluable across the whole spectrum, but the more advanced or complex active listening skills are called into use further across the spectrum and when trust is securely established.

The more advanced skills are usually called **challenging skills**. (Initially and, in some cases still, these skills were labelled **confrontation**. 'Confrontation' has many, rather unpleasant, associations, so that even though none of these was part of the counselling skill, the label 'challenge' is now more often used.)

> Recall a time, if possible linked to palliative care, when you felt challenged, and try to answer these questions:
>
> Your initial feeling(s) when the challenge came your way.
> Did you have any support?
> If so, was it a high or low level of support?
> How did the level of support affect your approach to the challenge?
> If you had no support (or a very low level), what were your feelings?
> How well do you think you met the challenge?

Here is a witness statement by an oncology nurse, talking about mentoring someone new to palliative care:

> *I'm determined to give her all the support I can. I don't want to smother her and she has to learn to manage these things, but you do need a lot of support. I remember the first time I was left with a patient who had just had a terminal diagnosis. The consultant had broken the bad news in a very technical way and I was just left to pick up the pieces. I don't think I handled it very well, partly because I was inexperienced (though in a way it never gets easier) and partly because I was just left. I often still feel guilty about that patient and it took me a long time to swallow my anger with the consultant. So you can see why I'm determined that my mentee won't have the same sort of experience.*

What this nurse's experience reminds us of is that if we challenge, we must be careful to provide an equal balance of support.

Challenge can, of course, involve people as well as particular incidents or events.

> Try to recall when someone challenged you (your actions, views or beliefs):
>
> How you felt about the challenger.
> Whether the challenge was of any use to you (at the time or later).
> How much you trusted the challenger.

These points need to be kept in mind when using challenging skills: the person we are challenging will probably have the same thoughts about us.

Challenging can often be seen as criticising or accusing, with a sense that the person being challenged 'should' or 'ought' to do something or that they should 'face up to...'.

There can also be a sense that they 'have to be challenged for their own good'. You will not be surprised to hear that this is not how challenging is used as a counselling skill. One reason is that criticising and accusing are severely at odds with the core conditions.

> List ways in which negative confronting would contradict:
>
> Empathy
> Genuineness
> Respect

Before we look at these so-called challenging skills more closely, and remembering the importance of self-awareness, ask yourself how you feel about challenging.

> Do you enjoy it?
> Why/why not?
> Does anything about challenging make you nervous?
> What, specifically?
> Are there some challenges which you avoid?
> Are you ever anxious that challenging will damage a relationship?

It is worth remembering two things:

⌘ Egan (1992) suggests that we have to earn the right to challenge, and that we earn that right by being prepared to be challenged ourselves (or, as one student bluntly put it, 'If you can't take it, don't dish it out').

⌘ Sensitively and supportively used, challenge can be a gift to help with opening up new perspectives and moving forward from 'stuck' positions.

The more advanced counselling skills which involve challenge are:

- self-disclosure
- immediacy
- advanced empathy
- recognising patterns and identifying themes
- 'concreteness'.

Self-disclosure

We have said that communicating in palliative care by using counselling skills should be guided by the principle of 'you talk, I listen'. It may be rather strange to see as a counselling skill something which involves the reverse. On the other hand, information giving is a helping strategy and if we have information or experience which would be useful to the patient or his/her relatives it would seem almost unethical to withhold it. On the other hand, too much of ourselves can be very off-putting. It was once the uncomfortable task of a trainer of bereavement visitors to withdraw one person because of complaints that, 'He just keeps talking about when his partner died'. In everyday conversation, we frequently hear comments like, 'I know just what you mean, because when I...' or 'I understand how you feel, because the same thing happened to me when...'.

This may not matter at all in the give-and-take of chat (although it can get very irritating), but it is not appropriate as a counselling skill.

> Link 'I do understand how you must feel' type statements to the core conditions and reflect on whether they are compatible.

Palliative care helpers, whether professional or informal, usually have a wealth of experience not only of practical issues related to death, dying and bereavement, but of the emotional or psychological aspects associated with the work. Sometimes it might be helpful to share this, but great care is needed to acknowledge the uniqueness of everyone's experience. As you look at the following example of inappropriate and appropriate self-disclosure, try to recall times when you have been helped when someone shared their own experience and times when you found it unhelpful or irritating.

Joan is a bereavement visitor who has a great deal of success judging from the feedback she receives from those she helps. Lately, she thinks that she is becoming close to 'burn out' and is feeling rather overwhelmed by the work. She tries to explain this to the co-ordinator of the bereavement service:

> *Joan:* I think I'll have to give it a rest. It's really beginning to get to me. Last week I found myself welling up with tears with the client and this isn't any good for them or me. I think it would be better for all of us if I just did admin. for a bit.
>
> *First co-ordinator:* Oh dear, yes it can get you down. I remember about two years ago going through the same sort of bad patch, but I kept going and eventually it all calmed down.
>
> *Second co-ordinator:* You seem to be going through a bad patch just now. Bereavement work can be like that. When it happened to me I battled on until it more-or-less went away, but I'm not sure if that's the best way to cope for everyone.

Here, you can see that the second co-ordinator is trying to show the bereavement visitor that she isn't alone in going through a bad patch, but there is no assumption that his way is the 'right' way to cope with the situation, only that it worked for him.

'Appropriateness' is the key word when using self-disclosure and we cannot know what is appropriate unless and until some level of rapport is reached and the relationship is established. Some guidelines for the use of self-disclosure are:

⌘ Use it sparingly.
⌘ Only use it when you know the person well enough to be sure that it is acceptable.
⌘ Don't stray into long descriptions of your experience — keep it brief.
⌘ Use self-awareness to be sure that the disclosure helps the other person, not yourself.
⌘ Be alert to any signs that by sharing something of yourself the client doesn't start to feel sorry for you as this would inhibit their disclosure which is the object of the exercise.

A word here about confidentiality. The BACP (1997) *Code of ethics and practice for those using counselling skills in their work*, makes two specific points:

❖ *Practitioners offer the highest levels of confidentiality consistent with their primary professional or work role.*
❖ *Any limits which apply must be made explicit.*

Within the parameters of our palliative care role(s) we should be clear about what the limits of our ability to hold confidentiality are. Some of us may have explicit codes of ethics or practice which guide us. On the other hand, as a student trainee once said rather ruefully to me, 'The trouble with confidentiality is that it's a one-way bargain'. He meant that the helper may promise confidentiality, but the patient or client need offer no such guarantee: 'I told my mother/son/partner what you said and they said...' is a not unfamiliar statement to many helpers. In relating this to self-disclosure we need to take care that anything shared cannot become distorted, or turned into gossip. This should help us to contain self-disclosure, and to be sure that we are using the skill only to help the other person.

> Make a list of possibilities which you would not disclose. Then reflect on any possible scenarios where it might be helpful to disclose them and whether you would do so.

Immediacy

Immediacy is a rather special form of self-disclosure which involves that rather over-worked concept — the 'here-and-now'. When people talk to as they may be talking about what they are experiencing now, this minute, or more usually, they will be describing something which has already happened and how this affects them in the present. The listening helper will try not to focus only on how the person felt, but how they seem to be feeling now. This is part of listening in 'the here-and-now', and is not as easy as it perhaps sounds.

> Sit with a book in a reasonably comfortable chair. What does the chair feel like? Is the fabric smooth or rough? Is your back fully supported?
>
> Change your thoughts to what is in the room — does everything please you? What would you like to change?
>
> Read your book. What are you now most aware of? The chair? The room? The written page?

As one thing (thought or feeling) takes precedence over another it becomes very difficult to stay with one. We have all experienced getting to the end of a paragraph and finding that we have not noted any of it — perhaps because of the chair, or more usually because our inner thoughts and feelings take precedence. This is why staying with someone else's 'here-and-now' can be so difficult: what they say or feel will resonate with our own thoughts and feelings and we can become distracted from their here-and-now.

Additionally, in any relationship, it is inevitable that two people will have thoughts and feelings about each other. As we learn more about the person we are trying to help we become more aware of our own reactions to that person and the reactions can vary enormously, and may sometimes be negative.

> Can you see how being genuine and also being non-judgmental could conflict here?

Read the following scenario (based on real experience) and reflect on how you might react (not respond) to the patient.

The patient is a thirty-six-year-old man receiving palliative care at home from the hospice team and the district nurse. He has several times expressed a wish to go to the day hospice, but when the volunteer drivers arrive he sends them away, even though there is a well-established procedure for not wasting volunteer time. He lives with his parents and seems to spend a great deal of time planning with them 'how much we can do the benefit system for' (his terminology). Although appointments for his visits are written down, he frequently has visitors at those times and expects the carers to wait or go away and come back later. He complains constantly about 'the poor service you lot give me'. He has recently had a birthday and his response to one of the home care team who commented on the number of cards he had received was, 'Yeah; I notice I didn't get one from you. I expect you thought I'd be a gonner by now, so you didn't bother. Got it wrong didn't you?!'

Your feelings may have reflected any or all of those experienced by the home care team; irritation, exasperation, annoyance, anger, hurt and all mixed with compassion for his terminal diagnosis and doubt as to whether his behaviour is the result of his illness, and some guilt around having negative feelings about such a poorly person. If none of these feelings is voiced, the patient has no way of knowing how his behaviour affects his helpers and so is unlikely to change. The difficult decision for the helper is whether sharing his/her reactions will enable insight in the patient or cause him to become defensive or even aggressive. If the relationship is sufficiently firm, the helper, aware of the dynamics between them and of his/her here-and-now feelings, might use the skill of **immediacy**. Immediacy involves not only being aware of our feelings 'in the moment', but being able to share these appropriately; 'appropriately' meaning non-judgementally and for the other person's benefit. An immediacy response to the patient in the scenario might be:

> *John, when you talked about birthday cards, you seemed quite accusing, as if you think I'm just waiting for you to die. I feel quite hurt about that. Perhaps it would be helpful if we talk a bit about how you see me and the team.'*

The helper is being honest about his/her own feelings, and is not accusing but inviting the patient to explore what is going on in the dynamic between them and, maybe, to clarify roles and expectations. The relationship would need to be well established before immediacy is used.

Think of a situation where you had or have strong feelings about something or someone and 'bit your tongue'. Did the situation change or improve? How do you feel about yourself? About the other person?

If a patient or relative is unaware of how their behaviour affects others, they have no choice about changing things; careful use of immediacy can create this awareness. It can also prevent our feelings seeping out in other ways, for example, distancing. Research seems to show very clearly that carers distance themselves from patients or clients about whom they have unresolved feelings.

> One way of 'testing' this is whether we avoid eye contact with the person. You might, in terms of self-awareness, like to monitor yourself for this.

The poem, 'The Poison Tree' by William Blake sums up this need, as a relationship develops, to express feelings:

> *I was angry with my friend;*
> *I told my wrath, my wrath did end.*
> *I was angry with my foe;*
> *I told it not, my wrath did grow*

As with all counselling skills, when and how we use immediacy is the key factor. We need to keep in mind that the objective is to help the other person, rather than to shift the focus to us and our feelings. In the scenario we used as an example, it would not be productive to make the patient feel guilty or angry by being complaining or accusing; on the other hand, if the feelings are not voiced the situation is unlikely to improve. Also, the cause of the patient's behaviour (which may be the result of various past bad experiences or general distress about his condition) will remain hidden.

> Remembering that immediacy is as challenging for the giver as the receiver, look back at the cycle of communication and consider how immediacy fits in to the cycle, especially at 'encoding' and 'interpreting' and feedback points.

Immediacy is especially challenging to the core quality of **genuiness and sincerity**. It is hard to be genuine if you are bored (the other person is telling you the same story, at length, again) or frustrated (once again the relatives have not done anything about agreed action) and this becomes a major block to active listening and relationship-building.

Advanced empathy is also linked to enabling the other person to develop new insights or perspectives and to deepen their self-understanding. As helpers, we need to have demonstrated that we are getting the person's message and hearing it from their frame of reference: once again the relationship will be well established. Advanced empathy tries to communicate with the hidden feelings, meanings and fears which are perhaps beyond the patient's immediate reach. The helper hears and sees the other person's perspective, but may challenge this by looking at alternatives or exploring the implications of the perspective. The most sensitive way of using advanced empathy is to express what is only implied, sometimes called 'playing a hunch' or 'sensing'. Here are some examples:

> *Mary, the problem doesn't only seem to be your attitude to the doctor any more; your resentment seems to have spread to the whole hospice team.*
> (Helping her to see the broader picture)

> *I'm sensing that you're rather more than disappointed about how your friends have reacted to your illness — you're also hurt and angry.*
> (Picking up on what has been expressed only indirectly)

> *Every so often you've just touched on some of the more intimate details of your care, but haven't said more. My guess is that you're finding this a very difficult area to explore.*
> (Opening up areas that are only hinted at)

> *From everything you've said, it seems that just now you really resent the restriction of looking after him. I realise you haven't actually said that directly, but is that maybe how you're feeling?*
> (Helping him/her draw logical conclusions from what was shared)

You will have noticed that all these hunches need to be expressed very tentatively. If we 'sense' something and decide to voice it to help the client, we have to be humble enough to acknowledge that we could be wrong, so being tentative is important. It is often a good idea to check out the accuracy of any hunches with something like, 'Am I on the right track here?' or, 'If I'm right, would it help to talk about that?' Being tentative is important not only because we could be wrong, but also because if our hunches are accurate the person may feel challenged at a very deep level. This can result in a release of emotion which may be cathartic and helpful, but could also cause a retreat or defensiveness. It will also be clear that time is important: if we have set some sort of time boundary and know that that time is almost over, it would be unwise to use skills which release feelings which cannot then be talked through at that time.

> Over a week, make a note of how your active listening causes you to 'sense' things.
>
> Did you voice your hunches?
> Why/why not?
> How challenged did you feel?

A further challenging skill, which may help to bring significant aspects into awareness is **recognising patterns and identifying themes**. Sometimes, active listening will disclose several themes or patterns of which the other may be unaware. There may be a particular adjective, always used in connection with one person for instance, which is significant; or the same person/situation may keep cropping up although the patient is unaware of this. Saying something as simple as, 'You've mentioned your mother several times...' can often be sufficient to highlight that something about the relationship needs to be explored. Or it might be possible to draw together several points which the listener hears as connected although the talker hasn't:

> *If I'm not mistaken, you've mentioned in different ways that you feel diffident about asking the doctor questions. For example....*

> *Perhaps there are some aspects of your treatment you need information about.*

Or,

> *... You're feeling perhaps a bit intimidated and that you'd like to be more assertive.*

> Think back over a conversation or interview you have had with a patient or relative (or, better still, over a series of conversations with the same person). Retrospectively, were there any themes or patterns? If you identify any, would it be helpful to bring them into the open.

Active listeners are often aware of themes and patterns, but hesitate to bring the connections into awareness. In palliative care these themes may be to do with pain, dying, bereavement, the after life, and the person may unconsciously be asking for help with these difficult areas, but unable to talk overtly about them. Communicating about such sensitive subjects is not easy for everyone. Our responsibility is to make the connection and allow the person to talk more or retreat, thus demonstrating respect.

The ability to pick up on themes and patterns is sometimes called 'connecting islands' — the listener picks up on apparently isolated pieces of information (the 'islands') and connects them for the other person. The use of an image to describe this skill, reminds us that using imagery is, in itself, a valuable counselling skill. 'It's as if you feel caught in a net and can't fight your way out'; 'You sound like someone at a cross roads where there's no sign post', are ways of demonstrating empathy, and can be especially useful in 'connecting islands'.

> If you have supervision or support or any other way of reflecting on your interactions in your palliative role, this is a good time to recall whether there are any 'islands' which you can help the patients to connect.

It is sometimes easier to master the challenging counselling skills and to see them as a positive, especially if we're diffident, or anxious that we may damage the relationship we've worked so hard to develop, if we view them as challenging **issues** rather than people.

> As you read the following examples of issues which could usefully be challenged, try to find a response (perhaps using reflection) which would challenge but not accuse.

'**Shoulds**' and '**oughts**' are often a serious block to insight or to attempting something which might help the problem or change the situation. However restricted palliative care patients and those closest to them may be by the illness, they do have choices. Challenging the 'shoulds' and 'oughts' so that they become 'could' is often very constructive. Here is a list of some 'shoulds' and 'oughts' that I have heard:

⌘ I know I should think about a will but...
⌘ I ought to get in touch with my father, we haven't spoken for years, but...

⌘ We really should try to talk about what he wants, but he won't open
up...
⌘ I ought to sort out the funeral but...
⌘ I know I should know what's going to happen, but I can't bear to find
out the details.

'Shoulds' and 'oughts' can also refer to the mysterious 'they': the people
who 'should' do something about the world conditions or the Health
Service or any other area of our lives with which we are dissatisfied.
'They' (the Government, God, the doctors, friends, family) 'should' do
something for change. This kind of blame is natural, but can prevent
personal autonomy. Helping the person to take as much control as
possible requires challenge.

> Next time you catch yourself saying or thinking something like, 'It
> makes me mad', try changing it to 'I allow it to make me mad'.

Challenging 'shoulds' and 'oughts' is important in terms of promoting as
much self-reliance as possible.

The past is a very good scapegoat. Many difficulties and problems can
be attributed to the past, and much present guilt is, obviously, linked to the
past. There must be few of us who, looking back, could not say, 'If only...'
about something: if only we'd worked harder at school; if only we'd stayed
in/taken that job; if only we'd married someone else; and so on. There is a
cliché that the one truth about the past is that it can't be changed.

This sense of 'if only' is often prevalent in palliative care: 'If only I'd
given up/made him give up smoking...' 'If only I'd insisted on a healthy
diet....'; 'If only I'd told him/her how much I love them...'.

Although the future for life-limited people may be drastically
shortened, we will not help them to make the best use of it if we do not
challenge their tendency to get stuck in the past. One of the most inspiring
statements made to me by a family with, at the most, one year of, as they
put it, 'borrowed time', was

> *We've been given a chance — what the Church calls*
> *'time for amendment of life' — and by heck we're*
> *going to grab it with both hands! Never mind what's*
> *gone, it's gone.*

This family did not need challenging on this issue, but others often do,
and part of holistic care is to offer the chance of change.

In the spectrum of helping strategies, we pointed out that enabling as much independence and autonomy as possible should be our aim. The sense of being a victim to the illness and therefore helpless in the fact of its onslaught or progression can lead to **passivity**. Challenging this can be a helpful use of counselling skills. This can be difficult when a very natural reaction of carers is to take over and to do as much for the patient as possible. Relatives or others close to the dying person may also experience a sense of helplessness, because hope for cure has gone. Our task in the use of skills is to help them see what they can do, rather than only what they can't. What is sometimes called the 'I'm useless; no good to anyone' syndrome is often helped by challenging strengths. This kind of negative self-talk is, in itself, debilitating and pointing out unacknowledged strengths can help towards a more positive outlook and enable a more pro-active and less passive approach, especially as far as relationships are concerned.

Challenging then, need not been seen as criticising or judging, but as a positive skill which helps towards new perspectives and greater autonomy.

There are, however, some people who present us with a particular challenge.

As you read the examples, try to imagine what response you would make and to identify the counselling skills you used in the response.

⌘ Some people seem to find it very difficult to stop talking. In a sense this could be regarded as a compliment to the helper — we have helped to 'open the floodgates'. On the other hand, going over and over the same ground to no real purpose except repetition may, after the initial catharsis, not help the person to move on. Knowing when to intervene sensitively so that we do not communicate boredom or irritation is not easy. Sometimes using imagery can be helpful: 'It almost feels as if you're wound up like a coil; perhaps we could both take a deep breath and work a bit more slowly'. Immediacy or 'connecting islands' can also be invaluable skills for intervening with a person who cannot seem to stop.

⌘ The other side of the coin is the silent person. Silence is rather difficult in some cultures — British culture especially. We seem to feel a need to fill it. We need to develop the skill of just being with the other person rather than 'doing' or feeling pressured to talk, especially if we get caught in the trap of filling silence with a question, which if it gets no answer leads to more (and more) questions. Careful attention to body language will help here. It is important to communicate that we are not uncomfortable with silence, and offering something like, 'You seem very quiet, as if perhaps you're having a conversation in your head. Would it help to share some of that aloud?' is probably sufficient. We must then, having challenged the silence, have the courage to wait. The nature of communicating in palliative care means that, as Wordsworth put it, there are many 'thoughts that do lie too deep for tears'. Also, the patient may be in pain, or tired, or the effects of medication may make talking difficult. All this needs to be kept in mind, but challenging silence is an important skill.

⌘ Some people seem to find some aspects of their situation especially difficult to talk about and as soon as the helper brings it up, they quickly move on to another topic, or smile and say something like, 'But that's not important'. This sort of avoidance can be rather frustrating for the helper who senses that it would be helpful to open up the issue(s). These issues are likely to relate to the wants, needs and fears which we looked at earlier, and so challenging the avoidance calls for great sensitivity. As with all challenging, it should not be attempted unless and until the relationship is firmly established.

> Look back over the three especially challenging issues and assess yourself for how comfortable you are in using skills helpfully. (If you think you are avoiding, challenge yourself.)
>
> The wound-up person
> The silent person
> The avoiding person

What does the word 'concrete' remind you of? What image does it summon up? Just as 'confrontation' has unfortunate connotations; so too does '**concreteness**' (of being set, or of ugly greyness). As a counselling skill, however, concreteness can be very useful in keeping both parties in a conversation focused. It is also a useful clarifying skill. For example, a vague expression like, 'Sometimes I feel worse than others', does not offer much opportunity to explore just what makes some times worse, whether there are any triggers or which times seem worse (or better). Using open questions, such as :

~ *Which are the times when you feel worse?*
~ *In what ways do you feel worse?*
~ *What seems to set it off?*

~   *Could you describe it for me?*

can help to make the statement less vague and our helping more focused. Concreteness helps people move towards being more pro-active and less passive, because it helps to prioritise exactly where distress lies. An example of where and how we need to be more concrete is in bereavement work where the phrase 'grieving process' is very common. To date, there are at least seven different 'grieving processes', so it is not a useful indication of how the person may be feeling. People are often termed as 'going through' this process (whichever one it is). What does 'going through' mean? How do we know they're going through anything? Perhaps it feels more like going round in circles? Concreteness can really help here.

> Try to formulate a response to these statements to help the speaker be more concrete:
>
> None of the staff really cares how I feel.
> Everything's getting me down.
> I hate going there — they're all stuck up.
> Social services is a waste of time.
> No one ever tells me anything
> Every time I try to do something, it goes against me.
> I'm no good at anything.

Open questions and reflection of meaning are both good ways of challenging people to be more concrete.

One of the ways in which patients or relatives challenge helpers is by asking for opinions: 'What would you do if you were me?' is one of the most popular. If we really believe that the goal is the other person's autonomy, we will be very careful in our responses to appeals of this kind. There is the obvious fact that we are **not** the other person, and expressing opinions can have a strong effect, especially on vulnerable people. We also need to reflect on the fact that if we do answer the question and our view turns out to be wrong we will have damaged the relationship: 'I followed your suggestion and now things are even worse'.

We are not talking about answering questions of fact, related to the illness, but to more existential questions to which there may not, in any case, be any answers.

Here are some difficult questions put to palliative workers. How would you answer them?

What will it be like at the end?
How bad will the pain get?
Do you think I should have the surgery or not?
They want me to go for respite care; what would you do?
Look — you know the ropes — will you ask the doctor for me?
Do you think I should tell him?
How long do you think I've got?

Challenging can be a real gift to the other person if it is used when the relationship is on a sound footing and used sensitively. If we avoid using challenge we can be depriving both ourselves and the person(s) we aim to help of a valuable opportunity to explore difficult areas or gain important new perspectives. In short, we will not be offering holistic communication.

To check your understanding of the work in this chapter, reflect (perhaps in a journal) on the following points:

1. On the helping continuum/spectrum, where do you mostly work? What counselling skills do you use? Would you like to enlarge the scope of your interventions? Why/why not?
2. What are your views about balancing challenge and support? Egan (1999) says, 'Challenge without support is abrasive', but he also pointed out that support without challenge can be rather bland. What are your views?
3. Confrontation is described in some dictionaries as 'to bring together for comparison'. How helpful is this definition in seeing confrontation/challenge as a counselling skill?
4. What dangers do you see in the use of self-disclosure and/or immediacy? Do they outweigh any benefits?
5. How could the five challenging skills facilitate holistic communication?

References

British Association for Counselling and Psychotherapy (1997) *Code of ethics and practice for those using counselling skills in their work.* BACP, Rugby

Egan G (1999) *The Skilled Helper.* Brooks-Cole Publishing Company, California

7

Removing barriers and monitoring interventions

An aspect of using counselling skills which follows naturally from the basic work of active listening and the more advanced work of balancing support and challenge is goal or target setting.

> Remind yourself of Weisman's model of an appropriate death.

The helper's task, using counselling skills, is to enable the dying person to meet these goals according to his or her own priorities and needs. If we are not aware of them we can make the fatal mistake of imposing **our** goals. This has sometimes been the problem with over-rigid interpretation of the Kübler-Ross model (1967; 1970): the goal of the helper has been, in the words of one professional, 'to get them through to acceptance'. If we are using counselling skills to facilitate the achievement of patient plans or goals, then we need to monitor carefully that the priorities really are those of the patient and that they should help autonomy.

> Reflect on how the core conditions would influence the setting of goals with terminally-ill people.

Self-awareness, once again, is crucial — we need honest self-appraisal about whether our belief that we are 'doing the right thing for the patient', is blinding us to what the terminally-ill person sees as their goals. In *Chapter 3* we quoted the *National Council for Hospices and Specialist Palliative Care* as saying that the goal of palliative care 'must be the best quality of life', for patients and their families. Views about 'quality of life' can vary enormously. Of course, even if we can divest ourselves of the view that 'we know what's best', some patients or relatives' goals may not be achievable. Balancing realism and idealism may always be a tightrope.

There are several criteria for measuring whether a goal is a goal, or whether it is more of a wish. The acronyms for these criteria are usually:

S   Specific, significant and stretching
M   Measurable (it should make a difference)
A   Achievable and an accomplishment
R   Realistic
T   Time constrained (set within a clear boundary for achievement).

> If a patient says his goal is, 'to improve my relationships with other people' would you say that it met the SMART criteria?

Perhaps you would agree that it is not very specific, for instance, in what ways does he want to improve relationships? With which 'other people'? A more specific goal might be, 'To share my thoughts and feelings about our marriage with my wife at least once a day in whatever time is left.'

An alternative acronym is:

O   Outcome orientated
S   Specific
C   Challenging
A   Achievable
R   Relevant to client values
S   Set in a reasonable time frame.

Most of the items on the OSCARS list are the same as those of SMART, with the significant addition of values, and this may be especially pertinent in palliative care, where helping patients, relatives and significant others to set goals, rather than only to express wishes, requires great sensitivity and will frequently involve value or belief systems. These values and beliefs may well relate to the concept of a 'good' death, or to issues about pain or to being in control.

Here is a list of wishes recorded by patients or relatives after a terminal diagnosis. As you read the list consider whether (using SMART or OSCARS sensitively) you could help to convert the wishes into goals. Reflect, too, on whether you would see any issues relating to values or beliefs.

- I wish I could be sure it will be painless.
- I don't want to be alone.
- I wonder whether they'll cope without me.
- I want them to know that I'm sorry.
- I want them to know that I really do care.
- It's important to me that my funeral wishes are followed exactly — how will I know?

- It's better if we carry on as if she's going to get better, she might.
- I wish they'd tell us how long.
- I can't bear the thought that they'll fight over my possessions. I've seen too much of that.
- I wish someone would tell me to 'let go'.
- If only he'd stop fighting.

You will appreciate that one criterion about goals — that they should be realistic — may be especially difficult to work with in palliative care and may require quite sophisticated use of those challenging skills (but who said using counselling skills is easy?). Often, the person knows that the wish is unrealistic; our task is to empathise with the emotion behind the wish and to help with prioritising, so that there is some sense of a positive move forward, however limited. Short-term goals may in themselves be therapeutic, because the sense of achievement promotes a sense of control. Attractive though goal and target setting may be it can present the helper with particular challenges.

> Try to list the challenges goal-setting may present.

In addition to the point about being certain that we are working to the other person's goals (even if we don't agree with them), **timing** is a challenge. It can be tempting to begin this kind of work very early in a relationship, because it seems so positive, but if we have not taken time to establish (by active listening) the particular needs of the patient or relative, we can find ourselves on the wrong tack. Goal setting almost always involves the use of challenging skills, as perhaps you found when trying to convert wishes into goals. Challenging skills should certainly not be used too soon, or too often in an interview or a relationship, and so goal setting, however urgent it may seem, is inappropriate as a first step.

In many areas of life and of palliative care it is seen as appropriate for one person to set goals for another and then, we might hope, to help them achieve the goal or goals.

> Draw a time-line and mark on it goals which have been set for you and those you have set for yourself and reflect on whether you have achieved them.

Research seems to indicate that people who set goals and work, however slowly, towards them, have greater self-esteem. There is also interesting research and case history evidence that the terminally ill who set goals seem to live longer. Many palliative care workers can testify to patients who decide to defy their prognosis and live until a wedding, or the birth of a grandchild or other more day-to-day goals — but the goal-setting seems to achieve a delay.

Goal-setting seems like a very worthwhile helping activity in which to employ counselling skills. When goals are set for people, it is usually someone in authority who does the setting. Sometimes this is appropriate and may be necessary.

> Look at this list of goals set by others and decide whether they are appropriate or necessary.

- ❖ You must keep taking the medication.
- ❖ Just take a few more steps every day.
- ❖ One day a week at the day hospice would make a world of difference for you both.
- ❖ You really should get the finances sorted first.
- ❖ Why don't we sit down and sort this out?
- ❖ The best thing would be to do it yourself.

> Try to find examples from your own experiences in palliative care of when goal-setting by others for a patient or relative was appropriate.

When we discussed the core qualities which should underpin counselling and the use of counselling skills, did it strike you that there is a strong sense that equality is a principle or value underlying empathy, respect and genuineness? Patients in palliative care and those closest to them frequently feel powerless and that others have all the authority. Think about the following quotation (Frankland and Saunder, 1995):

> *In every helping situation there will be questions of who holds power and authority, and having an awareness of, and dealing with, the central issues of power is an important, but often under-emphasised aspect of helping activities. The way power is handled may make all the difference between an act being experienced as helpful and having positive consequences, and its being experienced as well-intentioned, but meddlesome or even harmful.*

Nowhere is this issue of power more poignant than in palliative care, where the very people we are trying to help may feel totally disempowered. Paradoxically, this may make goal-setting as an equal, negotiated activity more difficult because patients feel so disempowered that they **expect** others to make and set goals for them.

We all have some kind of value or belief system which underpins the way we behave, especially the way we behave towards others. The values may be religious; The Ten Commandments, Love Thy Neighbour, the Koran: or they may be more sociological, 'Do as you would be done by'; or negative, 'Never trust anyone, then you won't be let down'. We need to be aware of our own belief systems and not to assume that they will coincide with those of the person we are hoping to set goals with. Our values and theirs could conflict. This is well illustrated by an anecdote related to me by a hospital-based oncology nurse, who had close links to his local hospice and often referred patients there:

> *I felt a fool. There I was singing the praises of St. — —*
> *— 's, and he said, 'No fear! They're all posh middle*
> *class types and I'm working class and proud of it!*

It is unlikely that people will work towards goals which do not resonate with their values.

Timing is critical in goal and target-setting, but timing of interventions is, generally, extremely important when using counselling skills; which skill to use when is a useful question to keep in the back of our minds, as long as it does not inhibit spontaneity or prevent us from being our natural selves — after all, ourselves is what we are offering our listeners, and awkward and stilted selves are not likely to be helpful. This is the difference between being self-**aware** and being self-**conscious**. The timing of interventions can be especially sensitive in palliative care, as there may be physical barriers associated with the illness (*p. 107*), and also the patient is at an especially vulnerable time psychologically. Buckman, whose work we mentioned earlier, suggests four particular areas of difficulty in relation to timing.

Patient (dying person)	Friend, relative, carer (you)
1. The patient wants to talk	You don't
2. The patient doesn't want to talk	You do
3. The patient wants to talk, but	You don't know whether/ how to encourage talk
4. The patient appears not to want to talk, but really needs to	You don't know what is best and don't want to intervene if it makes things worse

(This list could equally apply to a palliative carer and a relative of a dying person)

> **What question might you want to ask about Point 4?**

For me, the question would be 'how do we **know** the patient "needs" to talk?' Remembering about issues of power; who has decided that 'the patient needs to talk'.

The basic counselling skill of observation will be invaluable here, but we need to be sure that the person does or does not want to talk; perhaps they have just been talking to someone else, perhaps they are tired, or just don't want to talk today. Respecting this is important and, in a sense, is not confined to palliative care; we need to check that our well-intentioned willingness to encourage talk is not viewed as untimely or intrusive.

> **How do you ensure that your timing is appropriate?**

A Marie Curie nurse told me that one of the nicest pieces of feedback she had received about her care with timing interventions, was being introduced at a patient's funeral by the widow who said, 'She was great; she always said to him, "Do you feel like talking?" and never pushed it if he didn't.'

We may not realise how crucial such simple ways of assessing readiness to talk can be; overwhelming people with cosy friendliness or even praise (for all the other person knows, you may next start criticising) or being over-insistent about opening up painful areas, is invasive, may achieve the very opposite of what we hope for and undermine the other person's dignity. I once heard a helper tell a couple who were reeling from the news of a terminal diagnosis, 'Now, you **must** grieve'.

> **What is your reaction to this statement?**

There are many barriers to effective use of counselling skills for communicating with people in palliative care. In the dying person these may be physical or psychological. In close family or carers, the barriers may be mainly psychological, although the weariness and stress of caring can in itself be a barrier. Lastly, there may be significant barriers in ourselves.

Barriers created by the illness itself

Although we have talked about the success of communication as being, to a great extent, dependent upon the skills of the giver, perhaps success depends to an even larger extent on the capacity of the person receiving information or help to understand, and appreciate the 'message'.

> Remind yourself of the process from the 'wheel of communication'.

Nowhere is this more evident than in the breaking of bad news, when the shock of a terminal diagnosis may mean that the receiver(s) genuinely do not hear what is being said to them (although they often remember how it was said).

The greatest barrier for the receiver may be **pain**.

> If you have ever had pain of any kind, perhaps serious toothache, or as the result of a nasty fall, try to recall how this affected your ability to communicate.

Two of the mostly usually recorded effects of pain on communication are 'shut down', when people retreat into themselves, as if all their effort and energy has to go into containing the pain, so that there is none left over for either giving or receiving. The second reaction to pain seems to be irritability, even in those who are customarily placid and pleasant. It is as if pain in some way erodes some of the social skills which the years have built up, so that politeness and pleasantry no longer seem important. Sadly this irritability often shows itself most to those nearest to the person in pain, and can in itself create a rift.

Weakness is reported by eighty per cent of dying people. Weakness is often progressive, especially so in motor neurone disease, and although in itself a physical symptom, it can have a debilitating effect on emotions. Progressive weakness is both depressing and distressing, and the weariness is often linked to boredom.

Below is a list of other physical symptoms which can affect dying people.

As you read the list, try to evaluate the possible or likely effects of each on communication. Try to think about what counselling skills you might use to ease the barriers.

Breathlessness (dyspnoea)

A very frightening symptom, as people with even mild asthma will affirm, and very common in advanced cancer, and in progressive heart failure.

Loss of appetite

Dying people frequently lose interest in food, which can be distressing for carers who feel that proper feeding is part of good care. The loss of appetite may be related to the illness or to its side-effects, and eating itself may cause discomfort. Very often the loss of appetite leads to an alarming loss in weight, which results in distressed carers feeling almost that they should force feed the dying person. The psychological cause may be a better area for help.

Constipation

This is a well documented side-effect of drugs, and causes great discomfort. People in good health find constipation produces discomfort, lethargy and anxiety; how much more distressing must it be for the dying person? Yet it is a topic which, on the whole, we find difficult to talk about, and it can be a cultural barrier.

Nausea

'A fear that I may vomit is as bad as feeling sick itself, that's why I don't want to go anywhere or any one to come and see me, much as I'd like to', said one cancer patient. Nausea is also a side-effect of drugs, and may result from constipation. The anxiety it causes and the possible isolation is well illustrated by the patient's comment.

Fluid retention

This is extremely uncomfortable and can make the skin quite painful. For some people the unsightliness of swollen limbs can be distressing, especially when even gentle exercise, which might relieve the swelling, is impossible. This can be frustrating.

Confusion

Confusion, particularly if it leads to agitation, is distressing for everyone involved with a dying person and for the person him/herself it can be terrifying. 'Where am I?' 'Who are these people?' and even, 'Who am I?' are disturbing thoughts, and because the responses from carers often make no sense to the receiver, anger and aggression are the result.

You may be able to suggest a range of physical interventions which could help these conditions, for example, massage, provided that touch is culturally acceptable, could alleviate or reduce some symptoms. Here, we are thinking more about how physical symptoms may present barriers to meaningful use of counselling skills. Massage (an almost instinctive human activity) may enhance closeness and hence communication.

> Can you list other physical interventions which might facilitate communication?

Emotional or psychological barriers

If we look again at each of the possible physical barriers of which we need to be aware, it is not too difficult to determine how these can create emotional or psychological barriers.

Weakness

Here is a witness statement given to me by a young (thirty-three-year-old) father suffering from motor neurone disease:

> *It's as if every week I have to give up yet another thing that I've always done for myself without thinking about it. It's just wholly and totally depressing. And it's going to get worse: soon I guess I'll have to ask Helen* (his wife) *to do all those things my mother taught me to do for myself before I was three. And what is Alex* (his five-year-old son) *going to think of a dad who can't toilet himself? It's so humiliating. This illness robs you of a lot of*

*things but robbing you of your dignity is the worse
of all.*

Depression is one of the most difficult of all areas to work with, but it is also the most rewarding if our counselling skills can help to lift the mood even for a little, especially as depression can be very draining for carers: living with a depressed person is, in itself, depressing. The young father, and many other dying people who feel extreme weakness, also complained of boredom. This is an often forgotten aspect of weakness or perhaps we think that a dying person has too much to think about rather than too little, but listen to what one expert wrote:

> *Boredom can be one of the greatest problems for the
> terminally ill patient and a major cause of
> 'weariness', but it is often not observed by the
> doctor and family who are all so busy.*
>
> (Doyle, 1983)

He goes on to offer a range of practical activities which may help to alleviate boredom, but you can perhaps see how ensuring that there is time to talk about the patient's concerns might be the best possible way to lift the burden of boredom.

Breathlessness as we mentioned earlier, can be extremely frightening. When people are facing the imminent end of life, it is virtually inevitable that there will be speculation about how death will occur. Many people say that they are more worried about the manner of their death, than of death itself. A very real fear for many is that they will choke, or suffocate, and clearly extreme breathlessness can exacerbate this fear. Using counselling skills to elicit these fears can help to alleviate anxiety (and anxiety exacerbates breathlessness). Encouraging relaxation and using the skills to teach some of the techniques of relaxation can be helpful. It can also, if the activities are carried out together, reduce some of the isolation and loneliness which fear can bring.

Loss of appetite may well reflect the psychological state of the terminally ill person, and be linked to embarrassment about the possibility of vomiting or residual 'awkwardness' about discussing matters like constipation. In a survey of hospices in the UK, one of the commonest questions terminally ill people ask in relation to their death is, 'Will I be sick/vomit?' and for many this seemed to be the worst thing they could imagine themselves doing. The discomfort of constipation and resulting frustration often leads to embarrassment and fear, especially if the patient fears the intrusiveness of a rectal examination. Whilst there are fairly obvious practical 'solutions' to these physical problems (very small, frequent meals; laxatives, etc.), they will neither be recognised by carers as needed, nor acceptable to him or her if the patient is not helped to talk about them and this is where counselling skills can be so valuable. The depression and anxiety and even fear which results, especially in fastidious people, needs to be worked through in order for the practical solutions to be wholly effective. A word here about the difference between reassurance and genuine supportiveness.

> Read this witness statement to see how important it is to manage the difference between the two.
> The patient is a sixty-year-old husband with advanced cancer.

She does her best and I couldn't manage without her, but it's very difficult. I feel awful when I just can't face something I know she's taken ages to cook. And she's always saying she cleaned up after the kids when they were babies, changed their nappies and that, but it's no good. I don't want her cleaning me up, it's disgusting. And we've always been private about these things — it's no good her saying she doesn't mind; she's bound to and I definitely do. I feel so ashamed and it really gets me down.

The patient's wife may genuinely 'not mind', but clearly her reassurance is not convincing to him and seems to be causing him guilt and lowering his already fragile self-esteem. Counselling skills could help the patient to begin to view the difficulty from a different perspective, and might also help his wife to express her reassurances in ways that are more convincing for her husband. (You may be interested to know there was a positive outcome to this case history, where the hospice counsellor had been able to help the patient see that his wife regarded performing these intimate tasks as a privilege, especially as, as she put it, 'there aren't many ways left of showing him how much I care'. The patient was therefore able to be more accepting of her care because he could see that it was meaningful in terms of the short time left for their relationship).

Fluid retention may similarly be relieved by practical means such as gentle exercise, if that is possible, or massage, but how much more holistic these treatments are if they are shared activities (rather than 'treatment'), which enable and enhance a sense of closeness, so often a real deprivation for dying people. Good use of counselling skills, especially those of stage 2, can help to convert 'treatment' to 'activity'. One sceptical male carer told me how he had always thought that yoga was all about the lotus position, but that learning the breathing type of yoga with his partner who was dying of AIDS was, 'the best thing for both of us — I bless that teacher, tho' I really gave her a hard time at first.'

Sedation is often used to manage **confusion**, especially if the dying person is agitated or even aggressive or, if still strong, violent. Some forms of dementia seem to have abuse and violence as symptoms. Use of verbal counselling skills may not always be helpful to a confused person, as the terrifying loss of reality can make words seem meaningless.

> Remind yourself of the core qualities without which the skills are no more than technique.

The confused person needs to feel loved and accepted – continuing to 'be' with the person may be more therapeutic than trying to 'do' things. A clock, a calendar may help a mildly confused person, but may be meaningless to others, and our task may be to reinforce the reality of being accepted rather than the reality of what time or day it is. Confusion is distressing for carers, who may no longer be recognised or even may become the focus for abusive behaviours. Counselling skills can help by ensuring that the carer's self-esteem is not damaged by what can feel like unfair or even frightening behaviours. There is also the difficult dilemma of trying to ensure that self-respect and a degree of control are best maintained by sedation, as many carers feel a sense of failure about not being able to contain the person other than by drugs.

> Read the following brief case history and try to decide what counselling skills you might use.

The dying person seems no longer to recognise her daughter, her main carer, and is agitated and often hits out. The confusion may partly be dementia (she is eighty-three), although there had been no sign of this until secondaries of her cancer were treated. She may have had two minor strokes. The nursing home where her daughter feels very guilty for having placed her, takes great pride in its limited use of drugs. The daughter would dearly like to have a meaningful leave-taking of her mother — she realises how helpful this had been when mourning her father. The nursing home tell her 'not to worry – we'll calm her down', but she is worried because time is short and the urgency she feels is making it impossible for her to make any sort of decision about 'whether I should let her go, in a haze of drugs, or try to get through to her so that she knows that I'm there to the end — which I always promised. I don't know what's best for me, or best for her — what would you do?

The counselling skills you would use would help you to avoid giving advice or expressing your opinion; apart from anything else, even if you could decide what you would do in like circumstances, this would only be right for you. On the other hand, offering empathy and using reflection can help the daughter gain a realistic view and choose what may be the least worst option.

> In looking at physical and psychological barriers, can you list the benefits of an holistic approach to terminal care?

In working to remove psychological barriers, it is essential to have the core condition of respect. We all use barriers, to a greater or lesser degree, to defend vulnerable parts of ourselves. A terminally ill person is exceptionally vulnerable, and his/her closest relatives and friends are also at a time when they may feel extremely fragile. If we take away defences, we need to accept responsibility for what we will try to put in their place. Barriers, for some people, are a crucial coping mechanism and we remove them at our peril.

Barriers in ourselves

In *Chapter 2*, we looked briefly at how awareness of our own mortality can affect the way in which we communicate with dying people and their families. Elizabeth Kübler-Ross (1970) was convinced that we need to be aware of our own fears and anxieties, otherwise we will be in danger of projecting them onto others. Murray-Parkes (1986) theorises that we live in a world of assumptions — our assumptive world. My assumptions might be that I will outlive my parents and that my children will outlive me. I may also assume that of the four in every ten people estimated to die of cancer, I and those dear to me, will be part of the other six.

> How do you personally reconcile your 'assumptive world' with the need to be aware of your own mortality.

Several surveys of nurses have found that there is concern about a sense of inadequacy when professionals have contact with death and bereavement. A doctor commented, 'I am, of course, terribly upset when a patient dies, but of course I don't let the relatives see that'. Status may have something to do with this, but it may also be a fear of a relative's reaction: 'If I cry, you might cry, and if you cry I might not know what to do with your tears.' A fear of how others may react to news of impending death, or to discussion of death and to death itself may come high on the list of personal barriers. Here is a list of fears and anxieties about mortality, gathered randomly from people working in palliative care.

> As you read, take time to think through whether any resonate with your own anxieties and how you could ensure that you do not project them.

~ *If they choked I wouldn't know what to do.*
~ *I'd be really frightened if they had a fit.*
~ *To be honest, it's not easy if there's a smell.*
~ *I know cantankerous people are often like that because they're afraid or in pain, but it doesn't make them easy to deal with.*
~ *If you get involved you don't know how far to go.*
~ *There just isn't time to go into things deeply, so it's better to just chat.*
~ *Actually, I think most people would prefer me to be cheerful and up beat.*
~ *Being professional means not getting too involved.*
~ *You don't want to be morbid — things are bad enough already.*
~ *I'm afraid that after the death, the relatives will behave in a bizarre way.*

You might consider that none of these anxieties are yours, but they remind us that we would not be human if we did not have some personal barriers, which might affect our listening. Finding the right level and type of support to help us work through our anxieties is important.

The BACP (1997) *Code of ethics and practice for those using counselling skills in their work*, recommends that those who use the skills should have 'regular and formalised supervision'. The term 'supervision' can have rather unfortunate connotations — it has even been called 'snoopervision'. It is mandatory for counsellors, who would hardly accept it if it were seen as intrusive and punitive. It should be viewed much more as a time deliberately set aside for reflection on practice, and as support for what can be very stressful work.

> Draw a 'spider' diagram with yourself at the centre. Use the 'legs' to indicate those who support your palliative care work. Are you getting sufficient support?

Here are some of the benefits of supervision as defined by the Code. It can:

- ⌘ Offer a regular opportunity outside the line management system to discuss and monitor work, whilst still maintaining client confidentiality.
- ⌘ Help to maintain ethical and professional standards of practice.
- ⌘ Enhance confidence, clarity and competence in the work.
- ⌘ Develop constructive thinking about the work.
- ⌘ Help to recognise, manage and develop the emotional impact of the work in order to enhance effectiveness and prevent burnout.

As practitioners in palliative care, whether formal or informal, we take pride in our work and want to maintain it to the highest possible standards to facilitate that 'quality of life' for those we are trying to help. To achieve this we need to look after ourselves.

Informal support is invaluable, but it can be rather ad hoc. A time set aside regularly to discuss work in a structured way with someone where there is mutual respect can yield all the benefits claimed in the Code.

Being prepared to examine and monitor our work, implies a willingness to be accountable.

> In your palliative care work:
> Whom do you feel responsible to?
> Whom do you feel responsible for?

The BACP (1997) *Code of ethics and practice for people using counselling skills in their work* has this to say about accountability:

⌘ Practitioners are accountable for their work to both the client and the organisations in which they practise and their professional bodies.
⌘ Practitioners should therefore:
  • have received adequate basic training
  • maintain ongoing skills development and relevant learning
  • monitor their personal functioning and seek help or withdraw from using counselling skills temporarily or permanently, if their personal resources become sufficiently depleted to require this
  • take all reasonable steps to ensure their own safety, evaluate their practice, drawing where appropriate on feedback from the client, colleagues and managers
  • recognise the impact of their own beliefs and prejudices on the work they do
  • monitor their work to ensure that they are not discriminating against or disadvantaging their clients
  • consider carefully and exercise caution before changing the nature of the relationship with those who are or have been clients (eg. to a business, social, sexual, training therapy or other relationship) and consult with a supervisor or manager whether such a change is appropriate.

You will probably agree that standards like this are highly desirable to ensure that those of us who use counselling skills in palliative care work do so with integrity. The issue of accountability then raises the question of how we go about monitoring our use of counselling skills.

> Re-read the BACP Code's precepts about accountability, and reflect on how you do or how you could monitor your personal practice.

Here are some exercises which may help you to think of ways in which you could monitor your practice.

1. Think, in turn, of several people within your palliative care role who you have helped. How did you ensure that you worked with each person/patient in a non-discriminatory way? If you are confident that you were not discriminatory (eg. that there was no distancing from 'difficult' people) did you take into account social and cultural factors

impacting your client? How? How do you **know**? What feedback have you had about this?

2. How have you addressed confidentiality? What were your feelings (perhaps feelings of hesitation) about addressing issues of confidentiality? Who helped/could help you with difficulties?

3. Try the same exercise with regard to setting a time boundary.

4. How up-to-date is your theoretical knowledge in relation to palliative care? Do you, for example, know about some of the challenges to some well-worn models of grief? How will you ensure that you can evaluate theory? Who could help you?

5. How well do you work in a team? How do you get feedback on your performance as a team member or leader?

6. If you were using counselling skills, what signs of mental or physical distress would you see as beyond your level of competence? How would you go about referring? How confident are you in your data bank of referral people/agencies?

7. If challenged, could you **prove** that your work has integrity? How?

8. What do you know about the impact of your beliefs, biases, and prejudices on others? How do you find out?

To consolidate your learning from this chapter, try to answer and reflect on the following questions.

1. How would you define the difference between a wish and a goal? What skills would you use to help turn a wish into a goal?

2. How do values and beliefs affect goal setting?

3. What barriers affect the timing of interventions? How easy is it to use barriers as an excuse? When might it be acceptable to leave barriers, rather than to try to remove them?

4. How would you define the difference between 'supportive' and 'reassuring'? Are both interventions valid? Why? What is the effect of each on self-esteem? Could reassurance sometimes be an irritant?

5. What are your views about the BACP *Code of ethics and practice?* How helpful do you find the suggestions? Are they relevant to your work/role in palliative care? Could you 'sign up' to the Code? Why/why not?

References

British Association for Counselling and Psychotherapy (1997) *Code of ethics and practice for those using counselling skills in their work*. BACP, Rugby

Buckman R (1988) *I Don't Know What To Say*. Macmillan, London

Doyle D (1983) Terminal care and bereavement. *Medicine in Practice* **I**: 27

Frankland A, Sanders P (1995) *Next Steps in Counselling*. PCLS Books, Manchester

Johnson IS *et al* (1990) *What do hospices do? A survey of hospices in the UK and Eire*. Br Med J **300**: 791–3

Kübler-Ross E (1970) *On Death and Dying*. Tavistock, London

Weisman A (1972; 1984) *On Dying and Denying*. Behavioural Publications, New York

8

Endings

When we are using counselling skills, it is inevitable that we have an awareness of endings. At a basic level, this might be how to end a short time of interaction. We will want to be sure that the patient or relative or, indeed, colleague, does not feel left 'up in the air', or as if we have dashed off to something more interesting or more important. On a different level, there may be endings after a warm and intimate relationship has developed between the persons involved. There may be several reasons for ending the developing relationship: perhaps referral for some kind of specialist counselling, or there may be a move by either party. Carl Rogers (the 'inventor' of person-centred counselling) said that he saw himself as, '... a companion to my client, accompanying him in the frightening search for himself', which perhaps illustrates how significant endings are likely to be. In palliative care, of course, endings have a particular poignancy, as the work may and frequently does, end with death and bereavement.

> Try the following exercises to determine your own feelings about endings.

1. Recall a time when a person to whom you were talking began to show signs that they needed or wanted to be elsewhere. Perhaps they kept glancing at their watch or at a clock, or you noticed that they kept glancing away. What were your feelings?
2. Recall a relationship which was broken off by another person. Perhaps it was your first boy/girlfriend who decided that they preferred someone else, or perhaps it was a colleague who became 'cold' towards you or even stopped communicating altogether. Make a list of your feelings about the other person and about yourself.
3. Recall a relationship which you yourself broke off and the reasons for doing so. What are your regrets, if any? Are you comfortable or even glad about the rift?

Awareness of how we feel about endings will make us more sensitive to how others experience endings, and of how significantly a person's past history of endings can affect their interpretation of endings. This awareness can also help us appreciate why we may have difficulties in ending.

If we look at single 'sessions' first, what are the most difficult aspects? Here is a list compiled from members of a palliative care team, which included volunteer drivers and 'sitters', nurses, hospice administrative staff and some managers, all of whom agreed that they tried to use counselling skills in their interactions.

> ~ *Just as you're going through the door they say something earth shattering.*
> ~ *I couldn't go and leave someone in tears.*
> ~ *They don't start talking until it's time to go.*
> ~ *Sometimes a person has got quite angry when it's time to finish and said things like, 'Oh, I know you've got someone more interesting than me to see', or 'more important' or something. It can be quite hurtful.*
> ~ *If I know the death isn't too far off, I find it really difficult to stick to a time, even if I know someone else really needs me.*
> ~ *Sometimes you know something serious is going to crop up and there really won't be time to go into it and it's hard to know what to do.*
> ~ *Now and again too much comes out and you really think someone else ought to deal with it, but it seems too late to stop them.*

The poet, TS Eliot said, 'In my end is my beginning' and this might be rather a good motto for counsellors and users of counselling skills. If we get the beginning right, the end is more likely to be right too.

> What do you say about time at the start of an interview or discussion? How comfortable do you feel with setting any sort of time boundary?

If the person we are working with is under the impression that we have unlimited time, it is rather unfair if we then try to bring things to an end after ten minutes or half an hour. Learning to be comfortable about setting time boundaries is a critical aspect of using counselling skills, and the actual setting of the boundary is in itself a counselling skill. A useful way is to share the responsibility for time-keeping with the other person. Saying something like, 'We'll both keep an eye on the time...' can remind both parties that this is not an open-ended 'contract'. It can also help to add something like, 'I'll remind us when we're about halfway there, and when it's nearly time to finish'. Many users of skills initially find this boundary setting rather cold and feel slightly embarrassed about using the technique. Some helpers feel that it sets an interview off on the wrong foot and inhibits any building and developing of a relationship. These very understandable hesitations need to be set against the necessity of ending the interview well. For example, if we have not told someone that we have half an hour (or whatever time is available) to talk, and we also have to talk to someone else at the end of that time, we will not be able to listen actively as the thirty minutes draws to a close. We should not be surprised if the other person is hurt when we abruptly stop, and we will not have given the interview a helpful structure. If we look at boundaries from the other person's perspective it is, actually, more beneficial if s/he knows how long the discussion will last. There is the added bonus that if we have been clear about the time available, we need not feel guilty about ending at the given time. As with so many aspects of using counselling skills, 'it ain't what you say, it's the way that you say it', as the old music hall song puts it.

> Practise ways of setting time boundaries (on audio tape is good) until you feel comfortable.

In some ways the ending of longer-term work with patients or their relatives reflects the single interview pattern. We need, as the BACP *Code of ethics and practice for those using counselling skills* reminds us, to be clear about what we are offering, and perhaps to remind both the other person and ourselves about this from time to time.

> Remind yourself of the helping continuum, and of the range of helping interventions you may be offering.

We can agree that all of these can be enhanced by the use of counselling skills, and that it is important for all parties to be clear about roles from the beginning. Once again, the ending of a relationship which develops as part of the care given will be affected by the beginning. Outcomes are sometimes contrasted as **algorithmic** or **heuristic**. An **algorithmic** outcome is one which results from a predetermined set of objectives; determining in advance means that we have defined how and when to act under specific circumstances. An **heuristic** outcome results from a more uncertain process; we search for the outcome 'as we go along'. This process allows for greater independence and self-organisation.

> Review some of the endings you have experienced in palliative care and consider whether they could be categorised as heuristic or algorithmic.

You may have decided that each separate interview leans towards the algorithmic — there is a fixed time and there may be set tasks to perform. An overview of longer term work is perhaps more likely to lean towards the heuristic — the nature of illness and the varying nature of the patient's needs means that outcomes are less certain. The use of counselling skills to keep a balance between the two requires no small measure of skill and practice, especially as each person's history of endings will be so different.

> As you read through the following suggested model of an approach to endings, try to relate it to your own palliative care experiences.

Preparation

Just as with each individual session, it is helpful to prepare for endings. We need to use our counselling skills to talk about the ending and to engage with the process. We might need to use immediacy to acknowledge our own feelings of loss, especially if we have built up a close relationship with the dying person and his or her family or carers. If we are referring the person, this will need especially sensitive work, as it may be a source of resistance or even resentment. Some people's history of endings means that they feel betrayed and this makes preparation all the more important.

Disengagement

When we work closely with another person, particularly at a profoundly important time in their lives, it is inevitable that, for good or ill, some measure of attachment will occur.

> Remind yourself of Bowlby's theory of attachment (1972) from *Chapter 1* and reflect on how it might affect the way you approach endings.

Professionals are, of course, frequently reminded or even warned not to get attached to patients (or others for whom they may be providing care); even so, total lack of attachment is rare and too little can result in distancing.

> Reflect on your views about attachment; bear in mind the often quoted: 'the greater the degree of attachment, the greater the degree of loss'.

The image of being joined by a piece of elastic illustrates well the process of disengagement. The elastic gradually stretches as the process of disengagement takes place. The initial join may have been very tight, or not especially so, either way it is better to stretch the 'elastic' than to sever it abruptly. To achieve separation, the engagement with the process begun as preparation might need to consider what unfinished business there may be. It might also be helpful to review what family or cultural attitudes may be influencing the ending. If the ending involves a referral, it may also be necessary to think about new strategies for coping.

Separation

Separation can offer the helper a wonderful opportunity to model a healthy 'letting go'. Speaking about her husband's death, a young widow who with her children and the help of Macmillan and hospice nurses had nursed her husband at home said, 'I knew, really, that it was the end, but I kept struggling to hold onto him, and that wasn't good for either of us. Then one of the nurses said to me, "Just let him go" and that was wonderfully helpful; even though I didn't want to'. Perhaps the most useful modelling which the helper can provide is an acceptance that ending is inevitable and imminent. If we 'hold on' we are probably not helping the other person as well as we could. Working with the separation in a positive way is important, especially so if death is the separation. Counselling skills can make this process much more positive, in particular, skills of reflection and immediacy.

In situations outside palliative care, **'new horizons'** is often seen as the final stage of the ending process — the person being helped will move on to a different helper (referral) or may feel that they can now manage their problems autonomously.

> Can you think of ways in which the concept of 'new horizons' could be useful in palliative care.

A characteristic of 'new horizons' may sometimes be acceptance (the final stage, you may remember, of Kübler-Ross's model of dying [1970]), and an acknowledgement that work is completed may well be pertinent in palliative care.

If endings come about as a result of the need to refer, there are several considerations. Successful referral is a counselling skill in itself and may call for the full range of active listening and challenging skills to achieve. We need to be sure that we have a really good data bank of trustworthy people or agencies. You will remember that one of the strategies on the helping continuum was **inform**; giving information is a critical part of referral.

> What information could you give to:
>
> A patient worried about financial problems?
> A family wanting to plan a funeral?
> A relative who has no idea what to do after a death occurs?
> Someone with cancer; motor-neurone disease; acute heart failure (or other illness calling for palliative care)?
> What counselling skills would you use in giving the information?

Just having a list of names and addresses is not sufficient. Here are some questions asked by a hospital patient who was being referred to a day hospice:

- Is it easy to get there?
- When is it open?
- Is it free?
- What will they want to know about me?
- What will you tell them about me?
- What are the staff like?
- Are they all properly trained?
- What will they make me do?
- What if I'm ill when I'm there?

> Looking again at your own database, could you answer these questions, or similar anxious queries, if you were to refer?

The palliative care which you help to provide may have firm, helpful guidelines about confidentiality when referral takes place. It is often a serious anxiety for the person (whether patient or relative) being referred, and needs sensitive negotiation. Once again, 'in my end is my beginning' is relevant, as if no mention of possible referral and what it might entail has been made, the end will not be very satisfactory.

Difficulties with endings

There are some difficulties which seem to occur frequently with endings. One is often referred to as 'open door'. It is all too easy to say something like, 'I'm always here; I'll always listen'. Literally, this could hardly be true, but in a more general sense it is not a healthy modelling of 'letting go'. We may not think it kind or helpful to close the door with finality, but indicating that it's **always** open does not indicate 'ending'. It takes skill and courage to walk a tight rope between these two extremes, so that the 'door' is perhaps 'ajar'. If the person has been referred, it will not help the new relationship if they remain too attached to us, and could even create conflict. Self-awareness comes into play once again, as we need to be sure that we are working in the best interests of the other person, and are not holding on because of our own unacknowledged issues about endings.

Sometimes, endings can be made difficult by the finding of new issues, or even the creating of a crisis, in order to retain the attachment. This can happen if there is resistance to the ending. Ethical use of counselling skills demands that (BACP, 1997):

> *Practitioners are responsible for working within the limits of their competence.*

If we feel that the issues discussed are beyond our ability to help, or we do not have the time to work with them, then ending will be appropriate. But what if the other person does not agree and resists? Sometimes the resistance can take the form of avoidance — every time you broach the subject, the other person moves on to another topic. Or, it can take the form of an appeal which can be very flattering — it is very heart-warming if others feel that they want and need the relationship we have built up. Very occasionally the resistance can manifest itself as anger, which can be hurtful.

> What counselling skill(s) would you use in response to the following expression of resistance?

~ *Yes, well, what I really want to talk about is...* (after several attempts to broach the subject).

> ~ *But you're the only person who really understands.*
> ~ *I've never known anyone before who really listened to my side of things.*
> ~ *It's not very fair to leave me in the lurch, is it?*
> ~ *OK. Just go then; you've obviously had enough of me.*

Two things may help any guilt feelings we have in relation to endings. Firstly, if we have been clear from the beginning about the nature of the work then, however difficult the ending, we can feel that we acted with honesty. Secondly, we are using counselling skills for the benefit of the other person and if we feel, however reluctantly and for whatever reason, that it is in their best interests for work to end, we have the comfort of knowing that we acted with integrity.

Endings of single sessions matter and need to be structured into the overall pattern of the session if they are to be successful; endings of longer term work call for extra sensitivity, and we need to plan carefully and rehearse the skills which are needed. In palliative care, however, endings have a very special significance, because they are associated with the terminal phase of an illness, with death itself, and with the about-to-be-bereaved and the bereaved. As death approaches and when it is imminent, the importance of endings for all parties — the palliative care team, the informal carers or relatives and the dying person him or her self — becomes paramount. There may be many cultural observances, which need to be included as part of the ending. Dying people often need the reassurance that they will not be alone at the end and ensuring that this is possible (particularly if the death is in hospital or in a residential or rest 'home') can be a very helpful aspect of ensuring the best possible ending. There is also good evidence that a well-managed ending really helps the bereaved. 'A good end', as Shakespeare called it, really matters.

> Read the two following descriptions of endings.

A husband, whose wife died in a small Macmillan Unit where she had been moved from an oncology ward in a large regional hospital:

> *I was at home, having a bit of a rest and dealing with the dog, but the staff promised they'd send for me and I trusted them. So when they 'phoned, I went straight there and we pulled a chair up. I couldn't really hold her (I expect I'd have got into bed if*

> *we'd been at home!), but they got me extra pillows*
> *so that I could put my face next to hers. So I just kept*
> *touching it and telling her I loved her and to go, it*
> *was OK, I'd be all right. To be honest, I wouldn't*
> *have missed it for anything. And they did everything*
> *just right afterwards.*

A wife whose husband died in hospital after being nursed by the palliative care team at home:

> *We wanted it to be at home, where he could be*
> *himself, but in the end I agreed to let him go [to*
> *hospital] because of the pain, but it was hard to*
> *deliver him to strangers. Then I didn't get a call,*
> *and went in the next morning and the curtains were*
> *round, so I knew I was too late. I just can't seem to*
> *forgive myself for leaving him on his own, even*
> *though they keep telling me he wouldn't have known*
> *whether I was there or not. Now I know what ''Til*
> *death do us part' really means... and I wasn't there*
> *for it.*

What lessons can be learned from these two statements? Firstly, it seems to matter that there is some kind of pre-planning which all parties can trust. The physical and emotional needs of both the dying person and those closest to him or her need to be part of the planning. Even when the unexpected happens (as in the second case history, with the move to hospital), sensitive work beforehand can lessen distress. Good use of counselling skills will not only work on the goal of achieving the best ending from the other parties' perspective, but will also probe the 'What if...' scenario. Perhaps, had the widow in the case study been helped to explore, 'What if, for some reason, he has to be moved to hospital', the ending might have been less distressing for her. This is not easy work and, of course, depends upon individual circumstances, but preparation can be a great gift at a painful time. It is crucial when cultural and religious practices, deemed critical for a good end and to assist mourning, are involved.

> How much do you know about cultural and religious practices associated with death? How could you use your counselling skills to establish whether these are important to the people you work with?

An anecdote from my own experience may amuse you, whilst illustrating the differing views of people about religious practices. The dying person, a sixty-plus-year-old man, with a very robust style of speech, frequently said about his approaching death things like, 'When your time's up, it's up. That's it. You get what you get in this life, and it's the only one there is'. His wife was a devout Roman Catholic, which was a sort of running joke between them, especially if the parish priest came to visit. As death approached, the husband became very agitated and virtually ordered the palliative care team not to allow the priest in the house, 'Don't let that black bat anywhere near me!' His wishes were respected, and his wife reacted in a very mature way, secure in her own faith, but you can perhaps see practices could be a cause of conflict. The use of counselling skills to prevent conflict by discussing matters openly can help to ensure a better ending.

If death takes place in some form of institution, for instance, nursing home, or hospital, it can be very helpful if the procedures and practices are consistent and known to all parties. Here is a check list (which was prepared for hospital staff so not all items may relate to you personally):

1. Where do staff record relatives' and patients' wishes about what should be done and who should be called when death is imminent?
2. What is the procedure for calling close relatives to the bedside of a dying patient or informing them of a death? What training do staff have in doing this?
3. Do all staff know how to contact the police to ask them to break unexpected bad news? Do they give the police helpful information in such cases?
4. What training and information do staff have about different cultural patterns and religious rites in death and bereavement?
5. Do all staff know how to call someone to interpret for dying patients or their relatives? What training and support do interpreters have in carrying out this difficult task?
6. Are relatives left for as long as they wish with a patient who has just died?
7. How is the body left while it is on the ward? When are porters called to remove the body? How are bodies removed from the ward?
8. Is there a quiet room where relatives can talk and have a cup of tea undisturbed?
9. Are relatives offered the opportunity to speak to the appropriate doctor or nurse about the death and the circumstances surrounding it? Who makes this offer? Can relatives take it up at a later stage?

10. Are all relatives offered the opportunity to view the patient's body in the mortuary chapel or room? Who makes this offer? At what stage? Who accompanies them?
11. Are all nursing staff fully informed about the administrative procedures surrounding death and what relatives have to do? Do they have a simple one-page guide to give to relatives covering the necessary administrative details?
12. What arrangements do staff make if a bereaved relative is going back to an empty home? Can hospital volunteers be called upon to accompany a relative in such a case?
13. Who informs other patients in a ward or bay when a patient has died?
14. Who informs staff who were not there at the time of death?
15. Who is responsible for informing a patient's GP and, where relevant, the referring doctor, of the death? How and when is this done?
16. What is the procedure for packing patient's property and giving it to relatives? How are perishables and soiled clothing dealt with? Are patients' possessions given to relatives in an acceptable bag?
17. How do staff provide support for relatives of very ill patients who come into the hospital for a short time only and who may die suddenly? Do ward staff know how to mobilise health service and other resources in the community?

Once these sorts of questions are answered, so that a clear set of procedures is established, we need to use counselling skills to explain relevant points to the dying person and his or her relatives or close carers. This can take courage, particularly if hope of recovery is still present, or if there is resistance to talking about endings. An aim of palliative care is·

> *To create a support system for dying people, providing social, emotional, spiritual and practical care in an individualised way, enabling them to exert control, independence and choice, an opportunity to live as actively as possible and participate in decisions relating to managing problems. This might include negotiating the most appropriate place to die.*
> National Council for Hospice and Specialist Palliative Care Services, 1992

Where and how life ends is an important part of palliative care, and facilitating 'control, independence and choice' calls for a high order of counselling skills as death becomes imminent. One of the ways in which we can enhance endings is by trying to determine what the meaning of death is for each of the people for whom we are offering care.

> Try making a list of what you have heard people say about the meaning of death. You might start with, 'It's a happy release'.

Working to determine what makes for a meaningful death is part of the individualised care that we aim for. The significance of death will vary enormously from person to person.

Just as dying represents different losses for different people, so with death itself. The fears and wants and needs of each person about their end will depend upon many things, for example, pain, religious belief, finished (or unfinished) business. It would be sad if palliative care concerned itself only with the process of dying and not with the death itself. The time of dying can be regarded as a positive opportunity for sensitive use of counselling skills to ensure that the end is as good as we can make it, for all concerned, including ourselves.

Elizabeth Kübler-Ross's (1970) reminder that:

> *It is essential that everyone caring for the dying and their families understands... their own concerns and anxieties in order to avoid a projection of their own fears,*

seems very pertinent in this context: if we have not thought through how we want our own death (as well as our dying) to be, we may be in danger of making assumptions.

> If it is not too painful for you, try to think through what a meaningful end would be for you.

Here is a list of some of the issues about death given by a wide range of people; some may resonate with your own issues.

⌘ The place is terribly important to me.
⌘ I would not want to be alone.
⌘ I would not want anyone with me.
⌘ I only want the people I want there, not a whole gang.

- ⌘ I don't want people talking about me — I know from my work that some people seem to hear even when we think they're comatose or unconscious.
- ⌘ I want to be absolutely certain that someone will take responsibility for giving me Last Rites.
- ⌘ I'd like some music to go out to — music's always been a feature of my life.
- ⌘ To tell you the truth, I couldn't care less, as long as I don't know anything about it. Like at the dentist — they can pull my head off as long as there's no pain!
- ⌘ I couldn't go if I didn't know that the Last Offices would be done properly.

We can see from these statements that many people have strong feelings about their end. If we work in palliative care we need to have thought through what we would like at our own ending so that we can comfortably use counselling skills to encourage others to express their choices, and avoid the projection Kübler-Ross warned against (1969).

An especially poignant area of palliative care is working with children. Communicating with life-limited children can present difficulties as their verbal ability may be limited, and their concepts of dying and death will relate to their maturity. Additionally, the helper will need to be very aware that the dynamic will involve the child's parent(s) and that the goal of autonomy and self-reliance may be rather different from how it would be in adult-to-adult work. Parents of terminally ill children have great fear that they will suffer pain; helping both parents and children to understand and express these fears demands counselling skills of a high order and can be very challenging, particularly as we may need to use the advanced skills of enabling 'concreteness' (*Chapter 6*). For parents, their concern will be very general, whereas for the child the concern may be more specific, but their lack of experience or ability to express themselves may make it hard for them to communicate. A four-year old with a progressive malignant disease in a children's hospice said, 'I've got a bad toothache in my legs', which perhaps illustrates the kind of obstacle to direct communication that may arise. The professional carer will need a range of counselling skills, not only to be sure that they are really hearing the child, but that they are simultaneously hearing the parents' concerns. Dealing with fears about physical pain is not easy, but dealing with the emotional pain of both the child and his/her parents is even more challenging. A child's concept of death and its permanence will, of course, depend upon his or her maturity and will inevitably differ from the parents' adult understanding. The growth in specialist hospices for children is helping us to learn much more about both the physical and emotional pain of dying children and their parents. It has been noted, for example, that parents are often concerned firstly that strong pain relief means that there is no hope (this is a huge emotional hurdle for them) and secondly that if strong pain relief is given, there will be 'nothing left for later'. Good team-work will enable us to use counselling skills to communicate with the necessary clarity. Careful active listening will be needed to assess the parents' fears and hurt about their child's illness and death and to correlate this with what the child seems to know or be saying. (The following case study may be very distressing for you to read. It was given by the child's father, and illustrates how, often, children seem to be more attuned to their impending death than is thought).

> Mark was ten. He had mild epilepsy, which was well controlled with medication. He developed an operable brain tumour, and his parents were confident that the two illnesses were not mutually terminal. For several months before his death, Mark began to discuss funerals and informed his parents about the hymns he would like. He also showed them a plot in the village churchyard which he called, 'My space — close to that bench so that you can come and talk to me'. His parents had been a little dismissive and thought him a bit morbid, but after his death (of a massive seizure) they thought 'maybe he knew more than we thought; more than we did, anyway.'

Elizabeth Kübler-Ross (1970) postulated that we could learn much about children's awareness of their impending death by studying and talking through the meaning of their drawings; taking time to talk about drawings can be invaluable. A children's hospice nurse told me how surprised she was to learn from talking about artwork that many of her patients were concerned about body image. Younger children often had quite horrific fantasies about what their illness would make them look like; older children's fears were more realistic, but nonetheless painful. 'I don't want to look ugly/horrible/disgusting' was a common cry. Parents (and sometimes helpers) can see these anxieties as peripheral to the greater anxiety of the terminal nature of the illness, but for the children they are real and may also be a defence against the reality of death. Helping both viewpoints demands counselling skills. Research seems to show that dying children generally know that they have a terminal illness, and that often they try to protect their parents from distress. They know that if they talk about dying their parents will become upset and, for many children, seeing adults cry can be both strange and disturbing. A kind of conspiracy of protection, led by the child, can build up and the child may feel unable to express fear and be isolated.

> Try to evaluate your own feelings about this. Would you think it wise to explain to the parents? Would you 'go along with' the situation? What counselling skills would you use in either case?

A further complication in communicating with dying children, is that frequently there are siblings to be considered. Parents, already often suffering guilt that somehow they might be to blame for the illness (even though, rationally, they are not), may additionally be torn about anxiety for any brothers or sisters — which can range from to whom they should give attention, to trying to answer profound questions. If the siblings are older than the dying children their understanding may in itself create problems: 'Don't show him that you know' one fourteen-year-old was instructed. If siblings are younger their questions might seem naïve and hence irritating to already fraught parents. For the palliative care helper, trying to be a still point in such a complex whirlwind of different feelings is extremely demanding, highlighting the need for good supervision or support.

> Try to visualise yourself in the following (real) scenario, and imagine the counselling skills that you would need to call on.

Nine-year-old Daniel is receiving palliative care in a children's hospice, but he dislikes the unfamiliarity and misses his brother and sister and friends. He says he wants his 'things'. His parents try hard to be with him, but the other children have their needs and his father needs to work — bills still have to be paid. He knows that he is very ill, but not that he will not get better. The parents know that the illness is terminal, as do others. Daniel is very frightened because he has picked up that other children in the hospice 'go for treatment and don't come back' and he is due for invasive treatment, which in itself is frightening. He thinks he can't ask his parents: 'They keep telling me "you'll be alright"' and so he asks his main carer in the palliative care team, rather angrily, 'What's going to happen to me? Do you think I'll die?'

There are several issues here:

⌘ Have the parents given permission to disclose?
⌘ How mature is Daniel's concept of death?

⌘ What exactly has he 'picked up'? Communication comes from many sources and may be distorted.

⌘ Since Daniel's terminal nature is generally known, is there the possibility that he could learn the facts inappropriately, or from an inappropriate person?

⌘ What is the time factor in relation to treatment and ending?

⌘ What is the nature of Daniel's fears?

⌘ What hope can be offered?

Caring for a dying child heightens the natural conflict of palliative care; the conflict between the wish to nurture and show comparison and the deep wish to resist death. The sense of waste involved in the death of a child brings this conflict into sharp focus. The conflict can be stressful for the palliative carer, and there is some research which seems to show that if this stress is not well managed it can affect the care given to the dying child, often in the form of over-protection or over indulgence (Daniel's parents, understandably, constantly brought him expensive presents). Sometimes the stress leads to caring for only the physical needs, isolating the child emotionally, which is not the holistic care that is wanted.

Providing holistic care means accepting the stress, but being responsible about seeking and making use of good support and/or supervision. Endings, then, are a very significant aspect of good palliative care and repay thought and sensitivity. If we can think of them as a gift to the dying person and those closest to him or her, it will help us to prepare and to make good use of the opportunities that endings provide.

To confirm your learning from this chapter, reflect on the following points:

1. Why is self-awareness important in relation to endings? How can we develop our own awareness in order to be effective? What ways are open to you personally for self-development? Do you have a plan?
2. Find examples of how TS Eliot's, 'in my end is my beginning' could be useful in the practice of counselling skills. In what ways does the ending of longer term work reflect the ending of single interviews?
3. In what ways are boundaries important when using counselling skills? What are the difficulties in setting boundaries? How can you overcome any personal difficulties?

4. Terminally ill children appear to acquire information about their illness in steps or stages and from a variety of sources. What lessons can be learned from this? How did your own parents prepare you for death? What skills are needed to prevent distancing?
5. Working with dying children presents many stresses for both professionals and informal carers. What are the stresses? How can they be helped? How do you use your network of support?

References

Adams DW (1984) *Helping the dying child: Practical approaches for non-physicians*. Hemisphere, Washington DC

Bowlby J (1972) *Attachment and Loss (Volume 2) Separation*. Hogarth, London

British Association for Counselling and Psychotherapy (1997) *Code of ethics and practice for those using counselling skills in their work*. BACP, Rugby

Eliot TS (1968) *Collected Poems*. Faber and Faber, London

Goldman A (1992) *Care of the Dying Child in Paediatric Oncology*. Chapman and Hall, Medical, London

Henley A (1986) *Good Practice in Hospital Care of the Dying*. King's Fund Publishing, London

Kübler-Ross E (1970) *On Death and Dying*. Tavistock, London

National Council for Hospice and Specialist Palliative Care Services (1992)

Vachon MLS, Pakes E (1984) *Staff Stress in the Care of the Critically Ill and Dying Child*. Hemisphere, Washington DC

9

Bereavement support

Bereavement support in palliative care does not begin at the death; the weeks or months leading up to the final moment offer a valuable opportunity for preparation for bereavement. This preparation may vary from helping with practical details about post-death procedures (it is surprising how many people do not know how or where to register a death, for instance), to helping to plan the funeral, or the perhaps more emotional work of helping the 'about-to-be-bereaved' about how things may be for them after the death. In a sense, everything that we do for the dying person will affect the bereaved. Bereavement is a time of remembering and those closest to the person who has died will remember the quality and consideration of good care before the death and this will be a comfort. More importantly, the manner of the death will have a profound effect on post-death grieving. The reverse of this is that any insensitivity or perceived neglect on the part of palliative carers may be magnified and have a detrimental effect on grieving. There are many sad anecdotes of how the natural anger of grief may be exacerbated if, for example, there was insufficient information or if the moments immediately post death were hurried. More positively, if the time leading to the death was well managed and if the death itself and procedures around it were handled with sensitivity, the bereaved speak of the help this is to them as they mourn. It is important to see palliative care as, in part, preparation for bereavement. A stated aim of palliative care is:

> *To provide emotional, spiritual and practical care*
> *for the dying person's family and friends during the*
> *illness and after death* (bereavement care).
> National Council for Hospice and Specialist
> Palliative Care Services (1992)

We might consider that the emotional, spiritual and practical care which we give pre-death is inextricably linked to bereavement care — the two are not separate, but part of a continuum.

> What do you understand by the term 'anticipatory grief'? Try to
> write a short definition.

Anticipatory grief and its effect on bereavement grief has become quite a controversial concept, partly because the term seems to have acquired a variety of meanings. Sometimes the term seems to be used to mean that those experiencing anticipatory grief are doing so because they have a 'forewarning of loss'. Clearly, there is forewarning of death in palliative care but, as we have seen, the dying person and the about-to-be-bereaved are experiencing and grieving many losses from the time of the terminal diagnosis. Certainly we might agree that there can be a great deal of grief in advance of the death of a loved one. Sorrow in contemplating loss is very understandable. Would you agree with Kutscher *et al* (1969) who described anticipatory grief as:

> [the accomplishment of] *the most painful part of mourning in anticipation of the loss.*

This would suggest that we expect the bereaved to have adjusted to their loss **before** the death. Other writers (eg. Murray-Parkes and Weiss, 1983) consider that while a loved one is alive, it is not possible to grieve for them as if they were dead. Indeed, many people would find the idea repugnant — almost as if they were willing the person to die.

> From your own experience in palliative caring, are you able to deter-
> mine whether the grief and sorrow at the many losses experienced
> by a dying person and his or her loved ones could be said to
> 'accomplish the most painful part of mourning' or not?

A further consideration is that caring (if the palliative care is home based), or daily visiting for long periods, if the death is to be elsewhere, is exhausting. As one bereaved person explained to me, 'To tell you the truth, I really didn't have time to grieve. I was so rushed off my feet getting to the hospice, dashing home for the children, trying to cope with his mother... it was all I could do to keep running. Now I've just stopped'. This widow was perhaps like Brutus in Shakespeare's *Julius Caesar*, who in the heat of battle cannot mourn his friend Cassius, and says:

> *I shall find time Cassius, I shall find time.*
> Shakespeare, *Julius Caesar*, V, iii: 103

Uncertainty of prognosis can exacerbate this problem. Predicting just when a death will occur is hardly an exact science! Some patients outlive their prognosis by an astonishing length of time; others die well before the predicted time. Living with uncertainty is in itself a painful process and may be complex, so that, to quote Shakespeare again:

> *If it be now, 'tis not to come;*
> *If it be not to come, it will be now;*
> *If it be not now, yet it will come;*
> *The readiness is all.*
>
> Shakespeare, *Hamlet*, V, i: 232

The final line of this quotation is often contradicted by the many relatives and others who, when the death occurs, say something like, 'Even though we were expecting it, it was still a shock.' While it seems unlikely that the contradictory views about anticipatory grief can be resolved, some useful lessons may perhaps be drawn.

> As you read through the following points try to decide how you could use counselling skills to help with each.

- ⌘ That 'the readiness is all' may be an impossible goal, but there are many ways in which we can help to make the bereaved-to-be as 'ready' as possible.
- ⌘ Pre-death grief and sorrow may need as much support and sympathy as bereavement mourning.
- ⌘ Some people put so much effort into caring, or into helping the dying person fight their illness (and thus postpone death), that it is hard to see how anticipatory grief could be present.
- ⌘ The time leading to death, and the manner of the death itself, may be much more significant than whether there was, or was not, anticipatory grieving (however this is defined);
- ⌘ We should be wary of assuming that anticipatory grief will lessen the weight of bereavement grief. Creating some kind of 'hierarchy' or 'league table' of grief can be very dangerous, and is probably ethically unsound.

Bereavement has attracted the interest of many eminent writers, and various models of what has come to be labelled 'the grieving process' have resulted from this interest. Before we look at some of these, it may be worth reflecting on how long into a bereavement palliative carers could or should offer support. Some hospices offer bereavement visiting or continue to see relatives for some time after the death. Some offer group support, generally lasting from six to twelve sessions.

> Try to find out the practices local to you and in a wider context. At the same time, evaluate whether the extension of palliative care into bereavement should be time-limited.

In the language which seems to have grown up around bereavement, a commonly used phrase is 'letting go'.

> What does this phrase mean to you?

'Letting go' seems to have acquired a variety of meanings. Sometimes it seems to mean that attachment to the dead person should cease (perhaps within a certain length of time). Another meaning is that the bereaved should 'let go' of control of emotion. Yet another meaning is that the feelings associated with mourning (sorrow, anger, yearning) should be put aside or left behind. The way in which we interpret 'letting go' will probably affect the length of time for which we offer support. Some examples of how palliative carers and others have spoken about time-limited support and about 'letting go' are given.

> As you read, check the speakers' views against your own and try to justify whether you agree or disagree.

Time

~ *After the funeral it's time to take life up again.*
~ *It isn't like a cold, or the 'flu – it doesn't just stop; it goes on and on.*
~ *I think after six weeks, about, most people can carry on.*
~ *If we keep supporting the bereaved, how will we give palliative care to those still alive?*
~ *I think grief never ends, really, but it's only in the early days that I give support.*
~ *It's not really up to us* [hospice bereavement visitor] – *after the funeral, I ring up or something and if they seem to need support, I suggest CRUSE.*
~ *It's very hard, but the last thing you want is dependency. I'm not sure we should do more than attend the funeral.*

> ~ *Sometimes it all seems abrupt* [oncology nurse] *— one minute you're the carer and the next it's all over; you may not even be able to attend the funeral.*

As you can see just from these statements, ideas about how long palliative carers should offer bereavement support varies enormously. When we talked about time boundaries (*Chapter 8*), it was stressed that 'in my end is my beginning', and the need to be clear about time limits is just as important in bereavement care. If the organisation does not have any guidelines (and it might be a useful initiative to agree some), we need to be clear about our own time limits. 'How many bereaved people can I support?' and, 'For how long?' are questions that need answering. It is a delicate balance between, on the one hand, fulfilling the aim of providing 'emotional, spiritual and practical care... after death' (as we quoted earlier in this chapter) and continuing to provide holistic pre-death care on the other.

> How much support/supervision do you have to keep this balance?

'Letting go'

> ~ *'Letting go' means accepting that the dead person really is dead .*
> ~ *You have to let go of the past, because nothing will be the same again, and look to the future.*
> ~ *It means putting all those feelings aside (after a time, of course) and getting on with life.*
> ~ *Sometimes the emotions are so strong that you just let go*
> *— it's like a dam bursting.*
> ~ *Actually, I don't agree with all this letting go – I think you stay attached. It's just a different sort of attachment.*
> ~ *I don't know... the chaplain said that you have to let the dead go (to wherever they go) and that you shouldn't try to hang on to them. Just as the dying must, at the end, be allowed to die, in the same way the dead must be allowed to be dead – I mean we have to let them go.*
> ~ *'Letting go' means accepting reality; if you don't you'll never move on.*

It seems to be quite difficult to establish some sort of consensus about what this frequently used term actually means. This being so, it may not be helpful to use 'letting go' as any sort of marker or milestone as to when 'palliative' carers withdraw from bereavement support. Looked at from the palliative carer's point of view, there may be difficulties in 'letting go' of a relationship which may have built up over many months and become intimate at a very profound time. If this is so, the carer needs to ensure that healthy separation is sound practice, for both parties.

> Review the counselling skills that are necessary for 'letting go' in this sense.

Some of the thinking (and perhaps some of the confusion) about time in relation to grief and about the concept of 'letting go' comes from the models of grief and mourning which have grown up around the so-called 'grieving process', which the bereaved are frequently described as 'going through' or 'working through'.

> Take a moment to define what you mean by:
> * a process
> * the grieving process
> * going/working through the grieving process.

A recent literature search showed at least seven different 'processes', so it is difficult to find one definition. The idea of 'working through' also seems to indicate that whatever the 'process' is, it is seen as linear — some sort of road which the bereaved walk along. Yet many bereaved people describe their grief as something much more akin to going round in circles, which should alert us to the need to view each person's grief as unique.

One of the best known models of grief is Worden's tasks model (1983). The tasks of mourning in this model are seen as:

Task one

To accept the reality of the loss. After a death, even an expected one, there is a sense of disbelief. The bereaved find it very hard to accept that the loss has happened, is real and is irreversible. This disbelief can show itself in many ways, for example, laying a place at table for the deceased person, or planning to visit the hospice or hospital, although the person is no longer there. It is as if a curious tension exists: the bereaved know, intellectually, that the person they cared for is dead, but they so want it not to be true that, emotionally, they struggle with the reality. Except for some extreme cases of denial, this difficulty with accepting the reality of the death may serve a useful function, in giving the grieving person time to adjust and time for coping strategies to 'kick in' before the full reality beings to hit home.

Task two

Experience the pain of grief (or to work through to the pain of grief). This task requires the grieving person to experience fully the emotional pain of the loss and all the hurt that goes with it. The bereaved will suffer a range of powerful emotions, which may vary in intensity from day-to-day and hour-to-hour. Worden sees the full experiencing of the pain as an essential part of 'working through', and this view is shared by many. 'Bottling it up' or some other form of suppression is often seen as dangerous, although research into this is very contradictory.

Task three

Adjust to an environment in which the deceased is missing. 'Missing' is certainly a potent factor in grief and adjustment can be difficult and painful, especially if it is made unwillingly, as is usually the case in bereavement. The adjustments will have to be both external and internal. The learning of new tasks and responsibilities, especially at such a vulnerable time, will not be easy. In this sense, preparation may have been possible in the pre-death time. Learning to be a new 'self' may be even more difficult; adjusting to being widow/widower, orphan or other status may be the hardest thing to do. Trying to answer the question, 'Who am I?' can be very painful in bereavement.

Task four

To relocate emotionally the deceased and to move on with life. (Initially, Worden's fourth task was that the bereaved should withdraw energy from the lost one and re-invest it in another. You can perhaps see how this might have caused offence.) For some, this seems disloyal or impossible. There is also the difficulty that some people, the extreme elderly for example, or those with learning disabilities, have no opportunity for new relationships.

This 're-locating' means being able to find a new place in one's emotional life for the dead person.

> Using your experience of bereavement, how realistic do you find Worden's tasks model as a way of structuring grief?

A not dissimilar model is Parkes's phases model (1986), which describes four phases in the emotional reaction to grief. The phases are:

Numbness and blunting

This occurs immediately after the death and allows a brief space before the reality of the loss hits home.

Pining and yearning

A time of strong emotions, which may involve anger, denial and a range of other strong feelings.

Disorganisation and despair

The grieving person finds functioning and coping difficult and may wish to be dead themselves, even if suicide is not realistically contemplated.

Reorganisation and recovery

Life is taken up again and the grieving person begins to adopt the new self that he or she will now have to be.

There are many arguments against ordering grief into these rather linear structures. It is worth exploring what counselling skills might be especially helpful to support the bereaved in these 'tasks', or 'phases'.

Helping the bereaved to actualise the loss may be facilitated by using skills to encourage the person to go over (perhaps many times) the events leading up to and immediately surrounding the death. Describing the planning and process of the funeral may also help. This may sound rather obvious, but there is often kindly meant discouragement from doing this – 'don't upset yourself' – although the grieving person may need to go over and over these events. A listener who is prepared to accept, patiently, this need can provide valuable support. It may also help to use specific language. There is often a reluctance to employ words like 'death' and 'dying'. As CS Lewis said in *A Grief Observed* (1961), 'She has died. She is dead. Is the word so hard to say?'. We use terms like, 'lost' or 'passed away/passed on' and many other euphemisms. Using the actual 'd' word may help to reinforce the reality of the loss. Clarity of language is, of course, always important and may be crucial if we are using counselling skills with a grieving child. Euphemism to children about dying and death is very common, but it can confuse and cause anxiety, rather than shield from pain. Here are two examples:

A six-year-old: Mummy said Grannie's gone where there's no more pain. I want to know when she's coming back.

An eight-year-old: Grandpa had to have a special sort of sleep. I don't want to have one like that.

Here is what two writers about bereavement have to say about use of language. Do you agree with their views?

1. There are times when clear and precise language is of deep importance. Euphemism and evasions can cause confusion at a time when clarity is needed. The use of them can be particularly harmful for children, who do not have a grasp of the subtleties of language. They cannot distinguish the difference between 'gone away' on a holiday, to work or shopping or 'gone away' for ever as in death.

2. The legacy of not talking about death or talking about it only in euphemistic language extends far beyond the confusions created in a child's mind. It affects the treatment of the dying and is the cause of the linguistic evasions that so often surround a dying person. These evasions affect our attitude to life, for if we cannot acknowledge that life ends with death what then is the meaning of life?

> Monitor the language used in your palliative care team for whether the 'd' word is used. Reflect on whether its use helps to actualise the loss.

The second of Worden's tasks and the second and third phases of Parkes' model may demand the greatest counselling skills of all from the palliative carer: the ability to 'be' with the person's pain rather than to try to 'do' something to alleviate it. When someone is distressed, it is, for most people, very natural to want to do something to lessen the distress, yet often the depth of the distress means that we feel helpless and de-skilled. This can lead us into using the skills to distract the person from their pain. In the models we have looked at so far, **experiencing** the pain is crucial; the skills of reflection and of 'staying in the here-and-now' would help to avoid distraction.

> Look at the following lines and reflect on whether they express a certain truth about our willingness or unwillingness to stay with another person.

> *If you cry, I might cry*
> *If you cry, I might know I too am in pain.*
> *If you cry, I might feel self-conscious about my own*
> *difficulty in crying.*
> *If you cry, I might have to face the unpleasantness of*
> *my/your life.*
> *If you cry, I might not be able to maintain my pose*
> *of strength*
> *(or dignity, or composure, or whatever)*
> *If you cry, I might cry for all the pain in my own life*
> *and never stop crying.*
> *Therefore,*
> *If you cry, I will have to run away or shut you up to*
> *save myself.*
>
> Tatelbaum, 1989

Worden's task of adjusting to the changed environment (Parkes's fourth phase) often begins after the funeral. Many bereaved people record how they seem to have some sort of adrenalin rush, which carries them through the preparations for the funeral and the funeral itself. Then comes an anti-climax followed by the long, slow process of adjustment. There is some debate about this process of adjustment, which can be anything from learning new roles and tackling new tasks, to feeling able to do simple things like turning the light on at night to read without worrying about disturbing another. The debate seems to centre around whether those who have been involved in palliative care have, mostly, completed this task before the death.

> Consider whether you agree with this view and evaluate whether it links to your views about anticipatory grief.

While it may be true that some of the practical adjustments have been made before the death — as one patient said to me about her husband, 'I'm not going to die until he can cook himself a decent meal' — the emotional and psychological adjustment may not be possible. Learning to think of one's self as a widow or widower, not as a wife or husband is not easy. Seeing one's self as no longer a parent or as an orphan is a very profound transition. In some senses it is easier to help with the practicalities of adjustment, as long as we remember to help people become self-reliant, rather than 'taking over' and doing things for the grieving persons.

Helping the emotional and psychological adjustment may demand a higher level of counselling skills. Even so, the notion of promoting self-reliance is relevant. We cannot replace the dead person's place in the life of the bereaved, and should be careful to avoid any psychological or emotional dependence, understandable though it may be that the person needs a replacement.

We have considered the time span for which bereavement care could or should be offered. This is particularly relevant to Worden's fourth task. 'Relocating' the emotional investment made in the deceased is very complex and usually takes a considerable amount of time. In terms of self-awareness, palliative carers offering bereavement support will need to ask themselves two rather stark questions:

- for how long can I support this person?
- how can I ensure that the bereaved person does not 'relocate' their emotional attachment to the deceased inappropriately? Especially, how can I ensure that I do not become the new attachment figure?

There are several ways in which counselling skills can be used to help with each of these tasks and phases. (We have already mentioned accurate language). Accepting the reality of the loss may be facilitated by good active listening, allowing the grieving person to go over the circumstances of the death and to describe the funeral, perhaps many times. Because this frequently occasions tears, it is often avoided in order 'not to upset' the bereaved, but tears are a natural result of sorrow and can be healing. In counselling jargon, this is sometimes called 'giving permission'; this does not mean overtly saying 'It's OK to cry', but rather creating an emotional environment in which the grieving person feels able to cry, if they wish. This 'giving permission' is equally important for helping with task two. A common response to grieving people (and one which they frequently say annoys them) is, 'S/he wouldn't want you to grieve'. This may or may not be true, but it neatly avoids the fact that the person **is** grieving; implying that they should not be may be damaging, as it can add guilt to already existing emotions. The thought that they could be dishonouring what the dead want may be painful. Using counselling skills to allow the person to express grief and ventilate feelings is necessary if task two is to be achieved. Sometimes grief brings feelings which the bereaved feel are somehow 'bad', especially anger. Enabling people to see that feelings in themselves are neither 'good' nor 'bad' — after all, our feelings are what make our emotional selves — what matters is what we do with the feelings and how we can learn to manage them. Counselling skills can be the means by which people gain the insight to help them with this 'managing'. The core qualities, especially acceptance, which underpin the skills and which are communicated via them create a climate where the bereaved feel emotionally safe to explore a range of feelings which may be frightening in their intensity. Since Worden's model requires the bereaved to feel the pain of grief, staying with the pain rather than trying to distract the person from it is seen as therapeutic.

> Jot down the ways in which people are often well meaningly distracted. Try to work out why this might happen and how it can be countered.

Adjustment to the new environment — at least to its practical aspects — may seem an easier area to work with, but great self-awareness is called for. One of the strongest experiences in palliative care is the feeling of helplessness. The inexorable process of the illness and the sense that nothing can stop it can lead to an overwhelming sense of uselessness, frustration and despair. During the time leading up to the death, especially if relatives are not included in decisions and in as much care as possible, there can be deep levels of frustration. As one widow whose husband, after months of home care in which she had played a full part, died in hospital, put it, 'I was just redundant, really'. Similarly, after the death, the helper needs to take care not to de-skill the grieving person. It is a natural instinct to want to do something for people who seem so overwhelmed, but long term we may be contributing to, rather than helping to overcome, their helplessness. A good example of this has recently come my way from a widower whose daughters, son, and their partners 'took over' the funeral arrangement for his wife, their mother, until, he said (without rancour), 'There was nothing for me to do except to appear to be pleasant'. Some of the skills of goal and target setting may be useful, always remembering not to impose our goals.

Psychological adjustment to being a different self now that the person who gave the bereaved their previous identity is dead is demanding work. Skills that may be particularly useful are focusing and immediacy. Communicating advanced empathy will be reassuring — which is different, of course, from bland reassurance.

> Remind yourself of Elizabeth Kübler-Ross's model of dying (1970)
> (*Chapter 3*), which suggests:
> denial → anger → bargaining → depression → acceptance
> as the stages.

This model is sometimes used to chart the process of bereavement grief but like other stages or phases models and a linear approach, has recently come in for a great deal of re-assessment as to what actually happens in grief.

> Before we look at some of the more recent models, read this poem
> and reflect on whether it highlights the danger of seeing grief as a
> linear process.

The five stages of grief

The night I lost you someone pointed me towards
The Five Stages of Grief.
Go that way, they said, it's easy,
like learning to climb stairs after the amputation.
And so I climbed.
Denial was first
I sat down at breakfast carefully setting the table for two
I passed you the toast... you sat there.
I passed you the paper... you hid behind it.
Anger seems so familiar.
I burned the toast, snatched the paper and read the head
  lines myself.
But they mentioned your departure, and so I moved on to
Bargaining. What could I exchange for you?
The silence after storms?
My typing fingers?
Before I could decide, Depression came puffing up,
 a poor relation its suitcase tied together with string.
In the suitcase were bandages for the eyes and bottles for
  sleep.
I slid all the way down the stairs feeling nothing.
And all the time Hope flashed on and off in detective
  neon.
Hope was a signpost pointing straight in the air.
Hope was my uncle's middle name, he died of it.

After a year I am still climbing, though my feet slip
   on your stone face.
The treeline has long since disappeared; green is a
   colour I have forgotten.
But now I see what I am climbing towards:
Acceptance written in capital letters, a special headline:
Acceptance its name is in lights.
I struggle on, waving and shouting.
Below, my whole life spreads its surf,
all the landscapes I've ever known or dreamed of.
Below a fish jumps: the pulse in your neck.
Acceptance. I finally reach it.
But something is wrong.
Grief is a circular staircase.
I have lost you.

Linda Pastan, 1997

Concern that seeing bereavement as a sort of road with definable milestones along which a grieving person progresses has led to some alternative models. There was particular concern that terms like 'progress' could lead to a view that if people did not grieve in any sort of linear way, they were somehow not grieving 'properly' or were 'stuck'. Clearly this could make the bereaved see themselves as in some way abnormal, creating anxiety. While acknowledging that the models might be helpful to some people, there was a movement to look for models which might be helpful to others. This is why talking about the grieving process, as if there is only one, may not be productive.

> As you look at the following brief descriptions of these more recent models, try to consider:
>
> a) which you would feel most comfortable with
> b) how counselling skills would help you to work with them.

Stroebe and Schut have devised a duel process model (1995) (*Figure 9.1*). From studying the diaries of bereaved people from observation and from cultural consideration (in some cultures, for example, suppression of grief is seen as healthy, as is staying attached rather than 'letting go') she thought that people oscillate between expressing their grief and distracting themselves from it.

Figure 9.1: A dual process model of coping with loss (Stroebe and Schut, 1995)

The diagram suggests that when the bereaved are very focused on their loss, expression of grief, feeling the intensity of the pain (grief work) takes place. They may actively try to withdraw attachment to the deceased, and refuse to make any changes in their pattern of living — as if they hope by doing so that, somehow, the loss will not become real. On the other hand, they may at other times be more actively engaged in activities which are related to 'adjustment' and to 'reorganisation and recovery'.

> In what ways do you think the dual process model adds to the more sequential models?

In terms of offering bereavement support and using counselling skills, the model requires an ability to put aside a view that people be 'in' any one stage at any one time (and the possibility that they could be labelled as experiencing abnormal grief if they are not). The skill of reflection is important to communicate that we are accepting whether the person is currently loss-oriented or restoration-orientated: both may be necessary and are not necessarily sequential.

The view of grief as a road is also challenged by the many people who see themselves as 'going round in circles'. Trying to impose a linear model on people who experience grief in this way would not be experienced as helpful.

As you read the following case study, reflect on what sort of model would underpin the counselling skills you might use.

Liz is a hospice worker who supervised their bereavement service. This involved training the volunteer bereavement visitors, giving them support and supervision and accepting referrals herself if the volunteers felt their work needed more expert help. She also ran a series of bereavement groups for no more than twelve people, for eight weeks each. She then suffered a traumatic loss of her own, her ten-year-old son was diagnosed with a terminal cancer. He received home care, and some palliative care in a children's hospice (not the hospice Liz works for). She sought help after her son died and described her experience in this way. 'I thought I knew everything about grief — after all, Worden was my Bible — but nothing that happened (and is still happening) to me fitted any sort of pattern. I got so angry with people telling me (and telling myself) I was, "going through the grieving process". I knew very well that I wasn't going anywhere, if anything, I was going round in circles and getting nowhere. I just swung about from one feeling and thought to another; anything like a process would have been a luxury. Some days I'd think "Oh, I haven't cried today", then the next day I'd sob for hours. Nothing seemed to make sense. In the end I gave up looking for stages and all that, and just did whatever seemed called for. Now, to be honest, I think all this talk about "letting go" or "resolution" and so on just makes the helpers and counsellors feel secure, it has nothing to do with the bereaved and their grief.'

The concept of 'letting go' is for the most part based on Bowlby's attachment theory (1969; 1972).

Remind yourself of the details of his thinking.

Part of 'recovering' from grief was seen as breaking attachment to the deceased person. The image of a piece of elastic illustrates this quite well — at first the elastic which joins the bereaved to the dead person is so strong that it cannot be stretched very far. Eventually, it is possible to stretch the elastic further and further (just as a child, over time, becomes less attached to the mother figure). Several observers noted that in many cultures, the process of staying attached to the deceased is positively encouraged. Yet 'recovery' from bereavement did not seem to be in any way impeded. It was also noted that many years after a bereavement, some people in western cultures still feel very attached to the dead person, yet in no sense could they be seen as 'abnormal' as they were functioning perfectly adequately. They use phrases like, 'S/he will always be with me'; 'I can still hear his/her voice'; 'I think of him/her every day' and so on. These observations have led to a re-thinking of 'letting go', especially as the attachment theory is, in some senses, relatively new. Klass, Silverman and Nickman (1996) in their work on continuing bonds have been particularly important here. Instead, the focus has shifted towards how people can adapt their attachment to form a new relationship with the dead. This might accord with Worden's task 4, except that it is not the **end** of a process, but is active and on-going and may have begun pre-death as roles changed during palliative care. This new attachment is, in part, behind Tony Walters' model of bereavement and biography (1996).

> How well do you think you know the person to whom you are, or have been, most attached? Do you think that you know all aspects of their personality.

If I reflect on my parents, I knew them as their child. I did not 'know' them as husband/wife, even though I was, in a sense, an observer of their marriage. I did not 'know' them as employer/employee, and so on. I was surprised at their funerals by the many people who shared with me aspects of their personalities which were quite new to me. The funeral, and this general gathering of 'biography', is the opportunity to develop the new attachment. This contrasts very starkly with Jackson's view (1957) that:

> *Attempts to maintain ties with the deceased is a form of regression that should be discounted and discouraged. Regression is not cured by accepting it. It must be actively opposed, for it becomes worse if it is encouraged.*

> Reflect on this (rather extreme) view that attachment should be discouraged, and then reflect on whether memory, for instance (a powerful aspect of attachment) can realistically, be 'opposed'.

Disapproval of continuing attachment seems to have stemmed from a concern about the bereaved living in the past. The more recent thinking acknowledges that the bereaved will remain attached, that this is not psychologically unhealthy (or even pathological as was sometimes suggested), but rather an important aspect of adjusting to the new relationship which will develop.

In terms of counselling skills this is helpful, as the bereaved can be seen from a different perspective. They can be seen as engaging in the difficult and painful work of constructing new attachments rather than as struggling to sever bonds.

> Remind yourself of Marris's theory of loss and change (1974)
> (*Chapter 1*). Do you find an echo here?

As a final example of alternative ways of looking at grief, we look at a model which may have important implications for bereavement support. Because the pain of grief can be intense, it is often assumed that it diminishes over time. A study in New Zealand (1996) seemed to indicate that for some people the reverse seems to be true. Participants in the study were asked to describe: how they felt soon after the death; how they predicted their grief would seem after some time; and what actually happened.

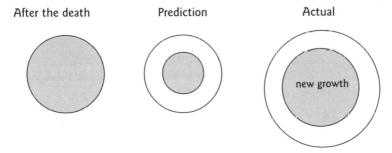

| After the death | Prediction | Actual |

new growth

What the diagram illustrates is that the bereaved initially felt 'all grief', and anticipated that over time they would stay the same, but that the grief would diminish. What actually happened was that the grief stayed the same, but that they had 'grown' around it. It has been observed that 'those who have lost much often have most to give'. The experience of grief can, of course, embitter, but it can also be an enriching experience, deepening compassion for others and revealing strengths which the bereaved did not know that they possessed. One widow, interviewed for this chapter, said:

> *Sometimes, of course, I do feel very angry and bitter*
> *about the unfairness of it all — what had he ever*

> *done to deserve to die so young? But if you ask me,*
> *a year on, have I gained anything from those*
> *terrible months then I'd have to say 'Yes, I'm much*
> *stronger now, I can do things I never thought I'd*
> *have to do, and I can really sense when other people*
> *are struggling. I think I was a bit unfeeling or selfish*
> *or something before. Not that it makes losing him*
> *any easier, it doesn't... .*

Her statement illustrates the New Zealand model very well.

The implications for support are interesting: we are able to empathise with the pain of grief while encouraging the bereaved in their strengths. We can think of this approach as not trying to offer the 'time heals' panacea (which many bereaved people find both insulting and irritating), but more that the pain remains, but that we get better at managing it — 'managing the heart' as is the bereavement custom in Bali. Counselling skills could then be utilised across the full spectrum of helping interventions.

A consideration of the role of support — particularly social support — in bereavement led Vachon and Stylianos (1988) to come up with the following two quotations:

> Read each and try to determine whether you agree, disagree or would like to qualify what they say.

> *Why should there be a need for outside help for a*
> *normal reaction like grief? It is not grief itself which*
> *is complicated, but the events that surround it.*

> *Bereavement is a social network crisis. The vacuum*
> *created through the loss of a significant*
> *relationship, especially in a closed network, will*
> *draw the whole group into distress. The joint*
> *experience of suffering may render network*
> *members unable to support the individual for whom*
> *the loss is the most immediate and profound.*

What the writers seem to be saying is that we perhaps tend to pathologise grief, making it 'complicated', when the real problem is that the normal support systems around the bereaved are inadequate. They are inadequate because network members too are bereaved. The logical conclusion is that 'outside help' is necessary. They suggest that there are four types of support which are most helpful to the bereaved:

> Reflect on which counselling skills each is likely to demand.

- emotional support
- moral support
- informational support
- practical support.

Emotional support

This allows the bereaved to express their feelings and being prepared to accept the normality of a range of powerful emotions. It may involve providing the 'safe space' where the grieving person can weep openly, if this is their need.

Moral support

This means steadfastly encouraging a belief that the grieving person will be able to cope (this is different from blandly offering the sort of reassurance which expresses itself in terms like, 'I'm sure you'll be all right'). It means enhancing self-esteem. (Several bereavement helpers have said that they find the DH Lawrence poem 'Song of a Man who has Come Through' a helpful inspiration for this kind of support.)

Informational support

This gives unbiased, relevant information which the bereaved seem to need. The unbiased nature of the information is crucial; we should not be projecting information about what we think the bereaved should or ought to know or do, but about what they could do. On the helping continuum, there is a great deal of difference between advice and information giving.

Practical support

This offers actual assistance. As we have already stressed, it is important not to de-skill the person and make them helpless. The practical support should aim to enhance self-esteem; indicating that someone is too helpless to do anything for themselves would be counter-productive. On the other hand, in the chaos of feelings which bereavement brings, some help with day-to-day tasks may enable a sense of control.

Overall, it seems that bereavement care or support is an important function of palliative care. Even so, there are some important questions, particularly about who should provide it (the person who nursed the dying person? Other members of the team? Trained volunteers?) and for how long it should continue. Bereavement support also raises issues about training for those who provide. It especially raises questions about, training helpers in any **one** model and whether this could be counter productive. A principle of counselling and counselling skills is that the person receiving help should be seen as unique, and this may be the key to answering the questions. That the relief of bereavement pain and suffering is a humane aspect of palliative care is true, what is important is that it is not applied according to rigid adherence to any one model.

To check your perceptions from this chapter, reflect on the following points and questions.

1. It has been argued that palliative care should end with the death (as is often the case if the death is in hospital). Try to make the case for and against this view, particularly bearing in mind resource issues.
2. Is the concept of 'anticipatory grief' particularly useful to palliative carers? There seem to be some dangers associated with the concept, try to define these and to think of ways in which they could be avoided.
3. Imagine that you are debating whether tasks/phases models are/are not preferable to other models of grief. Make the case for and against.
4. Which of the four types of support are you most comfortable with? In terms of self-awareness think how you could achieve a balance. Also, review how much support for each type of support you give, you are receiving (eg. via supervision).
5. Perhaps the most valuable of all counselling skills is **active listening**, and, as we have seen, there are many barriers to good active listening. Review the models of grief and the four types of support and try to estimate which present the likeliest barriers for you. How will you attempt to lower or remove them?

References

Boston S, Tresize R (1987) *Merely Mortal: Coping with dying, death and bereavement*. Methuen, London

Bowlby J (1969) *Attachment and Loss (Volume 1) Attachment*. Hogarth, London

Bowlby J (1972) *Attachment and Loss (Volume 2) Separation*. Hogarth, London

Cameron J, Parkes CM (1983) Terminal care: evaluation of effects on surviving family of care before and after bereavement. *Post-graduate Med J* **59**:

Jackson EN (1957) *Understanding Grief*. Abingdon Press, New York

Klass D, Silverman PR, Nickman SL, eds (1996) *Continuing Bonds*. Taylor and Francis, Philadelphia

Kübler-Ross E (1970) *On Death and Dying*. Tavistock, London

Kutscher A, Springfield K, Charles C, Thomas D, eds (1969) *Death and Bereavement*.

Lawrence DH (1958) Song of a man who has come through. In: Lawrence DH *Collected Poems*. Heinemann Ltd, London

Lewis CS (1961) *A Grief Observed*. Faber and Faber, London

Marris P (1974) *Loss and Change*. Routledge, London

Murray-Parkes C (1986) *Bereavement: Studies of grief in adult life*. Penguin Books, London

Murray-Parkes C, Weiss RS (1983) *Recovery from Bereavement*. Basic Books, New York

National Council for Hospice and Specialist Palliative Care Services (1992)

Stroebe M (1993) *Coping with Bereavement: a review of Grief*. Omega 26

Stroebe M, Schut D (1995) Helping the bereaved come to terms with loss. In: *Bereavement and Counselling*. Conference Proceedings, St. George's Mental Health Sciences, London

Tatelbaum J (1989) *The Courage To Grieve*. Cedar, London

Tonkin L (1996) *Growing Around Grief, Bereavement Care*. CRUSE, London

Vachon MLS, Stylianos SK (1988) The role of social support in bereavement. *J Social Issues* **44**(3): 175–90

Walter TA (1996) A new model for grief: bereavement and biography. *Mortality* **1**: 7–25

Worden JW (1983) *Grief Counselling and Grief Therapy*. Tavistock, London

10

Feelings, and other manifestations of grief

It has almost become a joke or a cliché that the question counsellors and carers using counselling skills most often use is, 'How do/did you feel about that?' It can be quite useful self-discipline to try not to ask it, but to take the responsibility for judging how the person feels from how they sound; those skills of active listening will often tell us how the person feels without the need to ask. Joke or cliché, it is certainly true that the major concentration in loss and bereavement tends to focus on feelings.

> Make a list of the feelings you think are the most commonly experienced by grieving people.

At the end of this chapter, you will find a set of charts which list the most commonly recorded feelings. Here we look at some of them before considering other ways in which grief may be experienced.

You will remember that Bowlby's attachment theory described a 'protest phase', during which a great deal of anger might be expressed as part of the distress associated with the loss. **Anger** is often experienced as a reaction to loss — both before and after a bereavement. Anger often results in blame, which may be rational or irrational. It would, for example, be very rational to feel angry that an employer's negligence had led to an illness which eventually results in death, especially if the death was painful. Anger and blame in bereavement quite often seem to be **ir**rational. As a widow described it to me:

> *I don't know who or what I was angry with, I was*
> *just angry. I'd march up and down and bang things*
> *— I think I was just sane enough not to break*
> *everything — and just be ANGRY.*

There have been several suggestions as to why anger seems present in so many people's grief. One suggested reason is that the person is actually angry with the dead person: the pain of loss is so great that there is a sense of, 'How could you leave me to suffer like this?' The grieving person feels diffident about acknowledging this ('S/he didn't want to die, how can I blame them?') and so directs the anger at God, Fate, the medical profession or any other convenient focus.

> From your experience of working with loss, try to find examples which might:
> a) support
> b) refute
> this view of anger.

A particularly difficult form of anger is when it gets turned inwards. Anger can be very disagreeable to be on the receiving end of, even when, logically, we know it is not directed at us. As a result of the reception the grieving person knows their anger is likely to provoke, they may turn the anger inwards. This 'internalising', as it is called, can lead to depression and to suicidal thoughts. An important aspect of bereavement care is to encourage expression of the anger. The core quality of **acceptance** to underpin the counselling skills is especially important. Trying to debate or argue about the rights and wrongs of irrational anger is, in itself, irrational. Letting the person know that the anger is not causing offence, and allowing its expression rather than trying to divert, distract or calm it down could be very therapeutic.

> What is your opinion of the view of some psychological thinkers that anger **must** be present in grief?

Helpers using counselling skills need to be cautious. In our willingness to 'allow' anger to be expressed, we can make assumptions that people who do not express it are somehow not grieving 'properly'. There have been reports (perhaps too many) from grieving people about well-meaning helpers who have virtually insisted that if they don't express their anger then they are suppressing it, or denying it, and this is somehow 'bad'.

As one exasperated widower explained to me, 'In the end the only person I was angry with was her (his bereavement visitor). I felt like throwing something at her, just to shut her up about it!' There is, after all, no law that says we must experience anger and if we claim to be accepting about present anger we should be equally accepting of absent anger. In terms of self-awareness we also need to consider whether what the grieving person does or does not express may say more about us than it does about them or their anger: 'Do they trust us enough to express what they feel?'

The two counselling skills likely to be most helpful are reflection and advanced empathy. These two are also helpful in working with another difficult, but very common grief emotion – **guilt** or self-reproach. There must surely be few of us who can say that we have always done as much as we could, always been as kind as we should, never been cross or irritable, never felt resentful (especially, perhaps, about the burden of care). These, very natural, human 'failings' – perhaps failings is far too strong a word for normal human behaviours – often become magnified in grief and lead to unhappy feelings of guilt.

> Look at these examples of self-reproachful statements given by the bereaved whose loved ones had died after palliative care. For each statement, try to think what your own response would be and which counselling skill(s) you would use.

~ *I blame myself. If I'd kept on at him, he'd have given up smoking.*

~ *I never encouraged him to take exercise, and so his heart just got worse and worse.'*

~ *I loved her to bits, but somehow I couldn't ever say it. Do you think she knew?*

~ *He was such a naughty child; tried my patience to the limit. Now I think I should have been more lenient with him.*

~ *If only I'd spent more time with her. I was always saying not now, or in a minute. Why was I always too busy?*

Once again, the quality of acceptance should underpin all responses. It is not helpful to tell people not to feel guilty — it would be wonderful to have some sort of switch which we could give to people to turn off unpleasant feelings, but reality is rather different. The sense of guilt is likely to be especially strong if the relationship which has now ended was in some way ambivalent (however much we love someone there is probably something which we wish they'd do or not do), but when the balance of love and dislike is uncertain, guilt can be heavy. Irrational guilt can often be helped, not by bland assurance, but more by widening the perspective. Helping the grieving person to focus on what they did do, rather than what they didn't do, is likely to be more therapeutic than the sort of reassurance that use phrases like, 'I'm sure you don't need to feel guilty,' or 'S/He wouldn't want you to feel guilty'— which may be true, but doesn't alter the fact that the grieving person does feel guilty. A sense of guilt may be a heavy burden in grieving children. Freud commented that when children say, 'I could kill you!' or 'I wish you were dead!' they usually mean it, rather than using it (as an adult might) as a sort of 'throw away' threat. If the person against whom the child expressed these thoughts does die, the child can think that they somehow caused the death and this is an extremely heavy burden to carry.

Read the following case study

Judy's brother had received palliative care at a children's hospice some distance from their home. Her parents spent as much time with Tom as possible and Judy frequently went to friends after school and felt that her parents' attention was always somewhere else, even when they were with her. She knew that Tom's illness was terminal, and sometimes found herself thinking, 'I wish it was all over. Why has it got to go on and on? If it was over we could settle down again'. After Tom's death, she is full of remorse, but is afraid to tell anyone of her thoughts, which she now thinks were 'wicked'.

This is a very great burden for a child.

Both anger and guilt can lead to feelings of **frustration** and **helplessness**. Most of us, if we feel we have hurt or upset someone, try to put things right by apologising or maybe offering them some kind of token that we are sorry, for instance, a bunch of flowers. The finality of death means that expressing regret is no longer a possibility and the sense of helplessness that this brings can be difficult for some grieving people, as well as frustrating. One of the factors which is known to affect grieving is the degree to which the person's self-esteem was linked to the deceased. 'I have no one to sanction what I do,' was the way this was summed up for me by a young bereaved father. This loss of a sense of self can create strong feelings of **anxiety**. Some of this anxiety may be practical, in the sense that the grieving person was dependent upon the deceased for a variety of day-to-day tasks. The time of palliative care may have helped with this although, paradoxically, the desire to help the dying person to feel as needed as possible may have meant the opposite — the grieving person may have been reluctant to take over any tasks and thus increase the dying person's helplessness.

> Look back at the types of support and try to think which would help most with anxiety.

Interestingly, many people who have no obvious practical concerns, seeming confident and competent about day-to-day practical or financial matters, nevertheless often express this generalised, unfocused anxiety. 'It's as if I've got to face an important exam or something'. This is clearly more linked to the 'Who am I?' question which we explored in earlier chapters. It has also been suggested that this more existential anxiety is linked to the greater awareness of our own mortality which bereavement (and, for that matter, all palliative care work) can bring. Sensitive use of advanced empathy can be valuable in helping this difficult and painful emotion.

> Work through the list of feelings at the end of this chapter and ask yourself how well you feel equipped to deal with each one and what counselling skills you might need.

'How do you feel about that?' has, as we mentioned earlier, almost become a joke in counselling circles. Certainly it is true that the focus of bereavement care has tended to be on the feelings — not surprisingly as these can be so powerful and overwhelming. While it is slightly artificial to separate feelings from other reactions, it is worth remembering that grief is also experienced **physically**, **cognitively** (in our thoughts) and **behaviourally**. For those of us wanting to use counselling skills, this is encouraging because it offers us more opportunity for helping.

The physical reactions to grief can make it seems like an illness.

> As you read the following witness statement, given by a bereaved mother, try to think what she would be advised to do about her 'symptoms' had she not been bereaved.

> *I feel sick. I don't want to eat anything, but I force it down because I have to. I keep on swallowing and swallowing. I drift about and get nothing done, but I get exhausted and breathless doing absolutely nothing. Sometimes I get the shakes and seem all of a tremble.*

Perhaps you would think that this person needed medical help of some sort and it may be that these strong physical reactions are, in part, what have led to what has been called 'the pathologising of grief'. This in turn has led to a strong lobby, stating that grief (except in very extreme circumstances) is not an illness, but a normal reaction to a major loss.

Try to decide, perhaps by listing 'for and against', whether you think that grief is a medical condition. To prompt your thinking, here is a quotation from Murray-Parkes (1986), which uses a medical approach:

People vary enormously in their response to bereavement. Some suffer lasting damage to their physical, mental, social and spiritual status. Some take bereavement in their stride... Risk factors are those predictors which can be identified at the time of a bereavement and are associated with good or bad outcome... they help us to identify people who are likely to have difficulties... and they provide us with clues as to the causes of good and bad outcome and the means by which these can be diagnosed. Risk factors have important implications for the prevention and treatment of pathological grief.

Other physical 'symptoms', as you will see from the chart at the end of this chapter, might all be seen as needing medical treatment if they were experienced by non-grieving people. Sometimes the physical sensations seem to replicate some of the symptoms of the dying person. Although there seems to have been little research into this, there is a wealth of anecdotal evidence from bereaved people who seem to experience the deceased's symptoms. This seems to be especially true of the breathlessness and nausea, so often seen in dying people. 'It's as if I've got a tight band around my chest, so tight that I can't get my breath'. This replication can be very frightening if the bereaved person sees good health as important, perhaps because there are young children or others who rely on them for care.

Physical symptoms combined with strong fear is a very potent mix, and we need all the counselling skills at our disposal to help. You may have heard about post-traumatic stress disorder, or critical incident stress. When people are de-briefed to help with this condition, part of the de-briefing sequence is to help the person see their reactions as normal: it is the traumatic event which was abnormal. You can perhaps use this strategy to help a bereaved person manage their physical reactions. Using reflection, we can help them towards the perspective that the death of a loved one (especially after a period of close, intimate care) is outside the normal run of experiences, it is unique, and it would perhaps be rather strange **not** to have powerful reactions. The skill lies in not **telling** the person this, but in using the active listening skills and, maybe, some gentle challenge to broaden understanding and perspective.

> Go through the list of physical reactions – your experience may perhaps be able to add to it – and review how you have used, or might now use, counselling skills to help with each 'symptom'.

Some time in the seventeenth century, the philosopher Déscartes pronounced, 'I think, therefore I am'; the meaning and implication of this statement have been debated ever since. Its main significance for counselling skills' users is that it highlights the fact that humans are thinking beings, as well as feeling and acting beings. Additionally, we can not only think, but think about our thoughts. It is interesting that if asked, 'How do you feel, now, this minute?' many people will respond, 'I think I feel...'; indicating that thought sometimes comes between some sort of stimulus and our emotional reaction to it. There are several counselling theories and therapies based on the importance of thinking and you might like to explore some of them for yourself (eg. Albert Ellis's rational emotive behavioural therapy [REBT]; cognitive behavioural therapy [CBT]).

For the purposes of using counselling skills to help the bereaved, we need to be aware that the thoughts of the person we are trying to help may be as important as the feelings. It is, of course, slightly artificial to separate thoughts and feelings as they are closely linked, although it may be helpful to enable the bereaved person to explore their thoughts. On a personal note, I have found that exploring what people were thinking at around the time of the death seems to be therapeutic. Sometimes it seems to come as a relief to disclose thoughts which might lead to shame or guilt. Trying to plan the practical details of the 'life that's left', and working out its financial aspects, for example, can result in self-blame: 'How could I have been thinking like that when she'd just died?'

> Remind yourself of Murray-Parkes' psycho-social transition model of loss and his views about the 'assumptive world' in which we live. Many aspects of the model are to do with thoughts (cognitions).

Most models of grieving seem to agree that a common reaction, particularly in the early days of bereavement, is one of **disbelief**.

Certainly it is difficult to adjust to the fact that all that made the dead person who she or he was is no longer present. Helping this sense of disbelief is one reason why there is much greater sensitivity about encouraging the bereaved to see or sit with the last offices and laying out, if this is culturally and personally acceptable. Even when this has been possible, there often seems to be some sort of dichotomy, with the bereaved person saying things like, 'of course I know that its happened, but I still can't believe it'. This can set off a chain of thoughts about where the dead person now is — and this seems to be true whether the bereaved person does or doesn't have a faith about the after life. Where are you? What are you doing? Are you okay? are very typical of the types of questions going through the mind of the bereaved, and helping them to verbalise these (without, of course, attempting to provide answers, even if we think we have them) can be good use of counselling skills.

The strongest question is likely to be 'Why?'

> Try to make a list of the 'Why?' questions a bereaved person might be thinking of; perhaps you have been asked or asked some of them yourself.

For the user of counselling skills, one of the most important disciplines is not to get caught in the trap of answering questions. Even if we think we have the answer to some of them, our answers are unlikely to be the definitive answer for the other person or to be very comforting for them. A Marie Curie nurse once said to her supervisor:

> *When he said to me, 'Why did she have to die? Why her?' I couldn't really think what to answer and I said, 'Well, we all have to die sometime', which I knew was stupid and the look on his face told me so, if I didn't already know.*

That 'we all have to die some time' is undoubtedly true, but it is hardly helpful to a bereaved person. Better use of counselling skills would be to empathise with the person's struggle with these intractable questions. Something more on the lines of, 'It sounds as if these questions are going round and round in your head and you're finding it difficult to get any answers', is more realistic. It also has the advantage of keeping the focus on the bereaved person, where it belongs; when we answer questions the focus inevitably shifts to us and our views and opinions. This is perfectly normal in day-to-day communication, but is not part of using counselling skills, where the objective is to keep the focus on the other person:

> *You talk; I listen*

not,

> *I talk; you listen*

Bereavement often seems to provoke so many thoughts that the grieving person loses track of them and becomes very **confused**. There is a sense that so much is demanding attention (at the same time as the painful emotions) that it is difficult to make anything coherent. For a person used to being able to think things through reasonably logically, this is disturbing. Some studies have shown that a helpful strategy can be to identify significant themes in their grief. This enables a less fragmented approach and gives a greater sense of control. In turn, this counteracts some of the feelings of helplessness. The other side of this coin, is that the thoughts are so all absorbing that the person becomes wholly **preoccupied** with them and perhaps forgetful of other concerns. The following case study, offered by a grieving adult daughter, illustrates this 'cognitive dissonance' as it is sometimes called. She is a legal secretary, working for the senior partner of a very busy solicitors' firm. She has lived at home with her father since her mother left the family home when she was fifteen.

> I don't know what's the matter with me. I find myself looking at the files at work and not knowing what on earth they mean. I can't even remember what I'm supposed to be looking up. It's the same when I go shopping — I end up with a trolley full of things I can't remember putting there and probably don't want anyway. All I seem to think about is Dad's funeral — I go over and over it. That, or I don't think of anything, just sit staring into space; my mind's a blank. It's just not like me.

A result of being wholly preoccupied by thoughts is that the grieving person can seem very withdrawn or even to be ignoring others and this can lead to a withdrawal of support, just when it is most needed. Patiently helping to explore the thoughts can be a valuable source of support.

A frequently reported manifestation of grief which is linked to thoughts is the **sense of the presence** of the dead, especially in the early days of a bereavement, when palliative carers are most likely to be offering support. Statements such as, 'I just caught a whiff of her perfume', 'for a moment I thought I saw him in the garden'; are very common. Most, but not all, people find these manifestations comforting, but are often diffident about discussing them in case they are thought mad. For children this experience may be frightening as belief in ghosts may be seen as 'spooky'. One explanation offered for this phenomenon is that we so desperately want the dead person back, that we, as it were, project them into our current lives.

> Try to think of ways in which you could use your counselling skills to open up this area.

It is sometimes possible to take the initiative and say that, 'some people think they see, hear or even smell the dead person, does this sound at all familiar?' If it is clear that it does not, then nothing has been lost if you move on.

It is interesting that both stress management and depression seem to respond best to cognitive behavioural therapy (CBT). Bereavement is, arguably, one of the greatest stressors any of us will have to 'manage', also, bereavement and depression share many features. This may be an indicator to us that if we focus only on feelings we may be missing many ways in which we could offer help and support through our counselling skills. An example of how thoughts can be a useful focus was noted in a study (Powers and Wampold, 1994) which observed that bereaved people often seem to associate not thinking of the bereaved with disloyalty or with somehow de-emphasising the importance of the dead person. Helping to understand that seeking relief from the anguish does not involve forgetting may be effective in utilising the thinking processes as well as the emotional.

> Reflect on a time when you experienced loss — not necessarily a bereavement. Try to recall what your **thoughts** were at that time.

Earlier in our work, we suggested that the four main skill areas are attend, observe, listen and respond. The way in which people behave in bereavement calls on our powers of observation.

> Take a few moments to list what you actually do when you feel anxious, angry, sad, frustrated, or any of the other emotions listed on the chart.

If we are to provide holistic care, we need to use our observation skills to note how each individual behaves. The individuality of behaviours is important, because one person may express anger by withdrawal and by breathing in a particular way, whereas another might express themselves more overtly by banging things or shouting or being very aggressive. **Sleep disturbance** and disturbing or distressing dreams are frequently reported. It may be worth noting here that the distressing **dreams** often relate to sexual feelings. It is rather sad that so much embarrassment seems to surround the sexual feelings of the bereaved. When we are distressed, we seek comfort, and comfort for many people will mean being held, yet the very person who could provide that intimate holding is the person who has died. Enabling the bereaved to talk about these problems, if they want to, can be helpful. One young widow said to me, 'Because you're bereaved doesn't mean that your body stops working... and wanting'. Self-awareness in the helper may be significant, as if we have prejudices about these matters, it may create barriers and prevent the other person disclosing. Sometimes nightmarish dreams are associated with the way in which the death occurred. Equally, many people have dreams which are happy and comforting, and wish for more, even though waking brings harsh reality.

Crying is the natural response to sadness and, generally speaking, it is not helpful to distract people from tears, although well-meaning comforters often do; for example, they avoid talking about the dead person because that might prompt tears when the grieving person longs to talk about him or her. Perhaps it says more about our inability to stay with tears? Some of the thinking processes or cognitions after a death may be to do with trying to find some sort of meaning in the loss. This may have to do with religious belief, or with a personal belief about the 'meaning of life'. We may be able to use counselling skills when people weep to facilitate this search for meaning. Tears will not always 'mean' the same thing – the person may be crying for the past, or with frustration or from regret, or for many other reasons. Exploring the meaning of the tears can help to give some sense to the often apparently meaningless suffering of bereavement grief.

> Try to recall times when you have cried or when someone you know well has shed tears. Were they always the same? What did they mean?

Sometimes the bereaved are themselves fearful of crying, 'If I start, I'm afraid I'll never stop'. Grief can often feel completely overwhelming and for many people the sense of being overwhelmed and in danger of losing control comes at just the time when they need all the strength that they can draw on. It is perhaps unfortunate that British culture, in the main, sees 'being strong' as not crying. Sometimes not crying even seems to mean being 'good'. It requires great sensitivity on the part of the helper to know how to walk this tightrope. Showing respect for the person's right not to cry, if this is important to them; communicating that it is acceptable and safe to let the dam burst with us; staying aware of our own attitudes to tears; all require counselling skills of a high order. Crying is complex and responding to it is equally so, demanding counselling skills that are finely honed and tuned.

A behavioural response linked to the dead person's possessions and clothes seems to have two sides. Some people seem to experience a need to get rid of all reminders of the deceased — wardrobes are cleared, photographs bundled away, items sold. Some psychologists have suggested that this is linked to guilt (rational or irrational).

> Try to work out why this view might have emerged and whether you agree with it.

Alternatively, experience may tell us that the reason for the behaviour may be linked to a fear that the reminders are so potent that seeing them, touching them, or even their smell will be overwhelming. Later on in grief, there may be regrets that few tangible reminders of the dead person remain. Once again, the helper has a tight-rope to walk: to accept the bereaved person's urgent need to clear away all reminders, but (being aware that longer-term this might be regretted) also of broadening perspective and understanding, so that the grieving person sees that remembering is not necessarily linked to external reminders. The opposite of the urge to clear away is the behaviour sometimes called **'shrining'**, where the bereaved person tries to keep everything exactly as it was when the person died — perhaps a child's bedroom is kept with kindergarten type décor, even though by now the child would be a teenager and not very interested in Bunnykins and nursery rhyme figures. Or, items that had significance for the deceased may be treasured for many years, even though they may have no practical use — a widow who kept her dead husband's golf clubs in the sitting room would be a typical example of this kind of behaviour.

> As you read the following case study, try to decide whether you see the behaviour as normal, morbid or acceptable.

Elizabeth and John had three sons. Mark, the middle son, died three years ago of leukaemia when he was sixteen. The family live in a semi-detached bungalow, which is a bit small for their needs, although each son had his own bedroom, although small. Elizabeth and John reacted very differently to Mark's death, although they agree that he was very well looked after by the children's hospice. Elizabeth was, at first, neglectful of herself and the home, but now seems to manage the household well, although she rarely smiles. John buried himself in work. They rarely speak about Mark because they fear hurting each other. Mark's room has remained exactly as it was when he finally went to the hospice after being cared for at home. A row has broken out: a visitor casually remarked that Mark's room would make a good dining room, or a sort of 'den' for the other two sons, one of whom said, 'Yes, Mum, why don't we do that?' Elizabeth is very, very angry, 'I could not bear to think of anyone laughing and joking in there. Why should they have a good time, when he can't? I'll never change that room.'

Margaret Stroebe (you may like to remind yourself of her imaginative dual process model of grieving) reminds us that 'shrining' may follow cultural patterns. In some cultures it might be dishonouring the dead not to 'shrine', and our own biases should not blind us to this. Culture plays an important role in how we grieve.

> How many cultural grieving practices do you know? How does your knowledge affect the help you can give?

In our day-to-day lives, if we lose something (car keys, knitting patterns, a watch) the natural instinct is to look for it. Many a parent must have responded, 'Look for it' when a child complains that some item necessary for school is mislaid. The word 'lost' is often applied to death: S/he 'lost' her mother/father/partner/child is probably more often used than the more explicit statement that someone has died. (Using the term 'lost' sometimes gives rise to the 'black humour' with which some of us working in this field seem to need to protect ourselves. At a recent training session a very caring palliative care nurse, impatient with euphemisms, responded to 'She lost her husband last year' with 'How very careless of her'. The resulting laughter was rather embarrassed... .) This term may have become so prevalent not solely because it avoids the 'D' word, but also because it accurately describes the sense of missing which is experienced by the bereaved. Supporting this view is the fact that many bereaved people seem to behave as if they are **searching** for something. Sometimes this will manifest itself by asking, 'Where are you?' (not always silently), sometimes by visiting places closely associated with the deceased, or needing very frequent visits to the cemetery or graveyard. 'I feel close to him/her there,' has been said to me many times. In young children this searching, which is linked to disbelief, may manifest itself as actually physically looking for the 'lost' person. They may go from room to room, as if the person they are searching for is perhaps playing hide-and-seek, or they may look behind or under furniture. This can be very distressing not only for the child, who cannot understand why the missing person cannot be found, but also for adults who witness their own distress played out in the child's search. There is still disagreement about children's concepts of dying and death and obviously the environment in which a child lives will affect how s/he perceives them: a child afflicted by war or famine will have a very different view from a child in a caring, comfortable environment. Even so, there seems to be general agreement that children's grief tends to show itself in behaviours; and these may be very disruptive, at a time when the adults around the child may be short of patience because their own emotional resources are already stretched to the limit by the death of the same person.

> Two-and-a-half-year-old Emily was very attached to her Grandpa who has recently died. Her parents have done their best to explain that she will not see him again and before her first visit to the grandparents' home have told her many times that he won't be there. Even so, Emily runs around the house and is disappointed that Grandpa is not in any of the places she looks. She keeps saying as she returns to her parents, 'Grandpa — no? Not here?' Her grandmother becomes increasingly distressed, the visit is cut short and the parents do not now know what to do about their next visit.

> What type of support might you offer this family? How could you use your counselling skills to avoid 'lecturing' them with explanations?

Some of the behaviours of bereaved children and young people can seem selfish, but this is rarely the case. Asking whether you can now move into a deceased sibling's room, or take over his/her collection of CDs is more likely to be an attempt to create some sense of normality in a world which may have been turned upside down since the terminal diagnosis. Adolescents have the additional problem of being poised between the worlds of childhood and of adulthood. They may be confused about whether it would be OK to cry (as a child might be expected and allowed to) or to be 'grown-up' and 'brave', especially if the model of grief around them is one of control. A bereavement helper can fulfil a valuable role, in seeing the family dynamics where everyone will be reacting in a different way and including the child or young person in the dynamic. A frequent complaint from young mourners is not only that they lack information ('What happens at a funeral?'), but that they feel excluded. A simple, practical gesture like sending a letter or card of condolence individually can be a first step towards inclusion.

> Try to compile a list of the types of questions children and young people might want to ask about dying and death. In terms of self-awareness could you answer them?

Although the lists at the end of this chapter separate bereavement reactions into four areas, and this separation is rather artificial, being able to intervene in a variety of ways can boost confidence and help us to be certain that we are not missing important areas which would help the bereaved. Ensuring that we get the balance right is probably what matters most. Perhaps the area most difficult of all is the spiritual, yet it is possible that this is where the greatest pain may be felt. A reluctance to offer counselling skills in the context of spiritual pain usually stems from anxiety that it might be seen as intrusive or, at worse, as an attempt at 'conversion' to whatever the helper's religious beliefs might be. This may, perhaps, be part of the difficulty — separating the spiritual from the religious.

> Take a moment to see whether you can write a definition of 'spiritual' and a definition of 'religious'.

Viktor Frankl, who endured the horrors of the Nazi concentration camps during World War II, but emerged with a depth of humanity many would aspire to, wrote, 'Man is not destroyed by suffering. He is destroyed by suffering without meaning.' The spiritual could be seen as a need to find meaning, and is concerned with ultimate issues of the value of life. Both before death and in bereavement this search for meaning may be powerful. When they receive a terminal diagnosis, the question for many people is something like, 'What's it all for? It's pointless, stupid,' as one patient expressed it to me. In bereavement, the need to understand the meaning of the death and pain of loss; the need to give meaning to the life

Before we look at these so-called challenging skills more closely, and remembering the importance of self-awareness, ask yourself how you feel about challenging.

> Do you enjoy it?
> Why/why not?
> Does anything about challenging make you nervous?
> What, specifically?
> Are there some challenges which you avoid?
> Are you ever anxious that challenging will damage a relationship?

It is worth remembering two things:

⌘ Egan (1992) suggests that we have to earn the right to challenge, and that we earn that right by being prepared to be challenged ourselves (or, as one student bluntly put it, 'If you can't take it, don't dish it out').

⌘ Sensitively and supportively used, challenge can be a gift to help with opening up new perspectives and moving forward from 'stuck' positions.

The more advanced counselling skills which involve challenge are:

- self-disclosure
- immediacy
- advanced empathy
- recognising patterns and identifying themes
- 'concreteness'.

Self-disclosure

We have said that communicating in palliative care by using counselling skills should be guided by the principle of 'you talk, I listen'. It may be rather strange to see as a counselling skill something which involves the reverse. On the other hand, information giving is a helping strategy and if we have information or experience which would be useful to the patient or his/her relatives it would seem almost unethical to withhold it. On the other hand, too much of ourselves can be very off-putting. It was once the uncomfortable task of a trainer of bereavement visitors to withdraw one person because of complaints that, 'He just keeps talking about when his partner died'. In everyday conversation, we frequently hear comments like, 'I know just what you mean, because when I...' or 'I understand how you feel, because the same thing happened to me when...'.

This may not matter at all in the give-and-take of chat (although it can get very irritating), but it is not appropriate as a counselling skill.

> Link 'I do understand how you must feel' type statements to the core conditions and reflect on whether they are compatible.

Palliative care helpers, whether professional or informal, usually have a wealth of experience not only of practical issues related to death, dying and bereavement, but of the emotional or psychological aspects associated with the work. Sometimes it might be helpful to share this, but great care is needed to acknowledge the uniqueness of everyone's experience. As you look at the following example of inappropriate and appropriate self-disclosure, try to recall times when you have been helped when someone shared their own experience and times when you found it unhelpful or irritating.

Joan is a bereavement visitor who has a great deal of success judging from the feedback she receives from those she helps. Lately, she thinks that she is becoming close to 'burn out' and is feeling rather overwhelmed by the work. She tries to explain this to the co-ordinator of the bereavement service:

Joan: I think I'll have to give it a rest. It's really beginning to get to me. Last week I found myself welling up with tears with the client and this isn't any good for them or me. I think it would be better for all of us if I just did admin. for a bit.

First co-ordinator: Oh dear, yes it can get you down. I remember about two years ago going through the same sort of bad patch, but I kept going and eventually it all calmed down.

Second co-ordinator: You seem to be going through a bad patch just now. Bereavement work can be like that. When it happened to me I battled on until it more-or-less went away, but I'm not sure if that's the best way to cope for everyone.

Here, you can see that the second co-ordinator is trying to show the bereavement visitor that she isn't alone in going through a bad patch, but there is no assumption that his way is the 'right' way to cope with the situation, only that it worked for him.

'Appropriateness' is the key word when using self-disclosure and we cannot know what is appropriate unless and until some level of rapport is that's left involve concerns with values and belief systems and may be said to be spiritual. A bereaved father explained this to me in this way:

> *I think its made me realise something I had never thought much about before — something quite profound for a practical chap like me. It's that when all our human needs are satisfied (warmth, food and so on) we need something more. I don't know what that more is, but I know that I need it. I'm no churchgoer, but I think I know something about the soul now.*

'Religious' is more to do with the practices some people employ to express their spirituality. The framework of ritual belief in God is the structure that facilitates the search for a meaning which transcends the material, for many people.

Facing death and bereavement may have real spiritual significance in the sense that they raise issues about the person's relationship with others, with him or her self and even with the universe. These issues can seem daunting, so it is not surprising that we avoid them, yet there is no doubt that many people do experience spiritual pain, especially if a person's view of life conflicts with their experience of it — terminal illness (especially if it was painful), loss, bereavement often bring about this conflict.

> As you read the following examples of how spiritual pain may arise, try to reflect on how you could use your counselling skills to help.

> *A person who has lived a life of strong faith in a particular religion, may wonder how God could let this happen. There may then be a loss of faith, just when the comfort of religion may be most needed.*

> *Someone who placed great faith in science and medicine may be bitterly disappointed that when it came to his/her personal need, it let them down.*

> *A philosophy that the material world is all that there is may be deeply rocked by asking 'Why me/us?' when the logical question would be, 'Why not me?'*

If we have the courage to help with spiritual pain, it may be helpful to know some of the indicators so that we can provide a climate of safety, should the person wish to explore this aspect of their loss. Some suggestions of how spiritual pain may manifest have been offered by palliative care workers, especially hospice and hospital chaplains. You may be able to add to them, from your personal experience.

- A break with religious/cultural ties, eg. 'I don't believe in God any more; I can't ask for help.' (Presumably via prayer?)
- Sense of meaninglessness/hopelessness manifesting as cynicism; suicidal feelings; apathy and withdrawal.
- Sense of guilt and shame — the illness and death are a form of punishment. The person may feel unworthy and unacceptable (to others, to themselves or to God). In turn, this can lead to general bitterness and an unforgiving attitude to self and others.
- A loss of control, as if the person thinks, 'If there's no meaning, I might as well do what I like', leading to extreme and sometimes self-destructive behaviours (abusing alcohol or other drugs).
- Intense questioning and a sense of not being able to endure the suffering. In the terminally ill, this may result in requests for euthanasia; in the bereaved, a wish to 'end it all'.
- Fear of mortality.
- Undue stoicism, as if the person is so determined not to be concerned about 'the meaning of life' that they virtually become an automaton.

Spiritual pain may be one of the most difficult areas to work with, but if we can be clear about our own views, about the difference between the spiritual and the religious, and humble enough to acknowledge that there are no universal answers to this profound search for meaning, it can be very rewarding. It is also, perhaps, the work which binds or encompasses the other four areas we looked at.

Instead of the usual review questions at the end of this chapter, you might like to fill in the following chart, which has been adapted from one used to gauge nurses' reactions to working with the bereaved.

How difficult would you find it to deal with the following responses to bereavement?

Response		Difficult to cope with	Manageable	No problem
Denial	of facts or reality			
Acceptance	'That's life' 'We all have to die'			
Anger	directed at you, staff, God, self			
Withdrawal	Inaccessible; silent; not wishing/willing to enter into any form of dialogue			
Inappropriate	Laughing; wildly over-active; distracting self by seeking new relation-ships			
Crying	Racked by sobs			
Questioning	Why? (search for meaning)			
Guilt				
Abuse	Alcohol; drugs; over/under-eating			

Physical

'Hollowness' in stomach			
A tight chest			
A tight throat			
Being over sensitive to noise			
Breathlessness			
Weakness in the muscles ('shakiness')			
Fatigue and lack of energy			
Dry mouth/urge to keep swallowing			
Nausea			
Pain ('as if my insides were being torn out')			
Your own examples			

Emotional
Sadness
Anger (vengeful)
Frustration
Guilt and self-reproach
Anxiety and fear
Loneliness
'Aloneness' (isolated from others)
Helplessness
Shock (dazed)
Numbness
Overwhelmed
Relief
Calm
Yearning/pining
Insecure/vulnerable
Worthless
Sense of being punished
Need to be held
Your own examples

Cognitive
Disbelief
Confusion
Preoccupation
Sense of presence
Why?
Forgetful
Your own examples

Behavioural
Sleep disturbance
Behaviour disturbance (eating, drinking)
Social withdrawal
Dreams/nightmares
Avoidance of reminders
Searching or calling out
Visiting
Sighing
Restlessness of over-acting
Crying
Your own examples

References

Bowlby J (1969) *Attachment and Loss (Volume 1) Attachment.* Hogarth, London

Bowlby J (1972) *Attachment and Loss (Volume 2) Separation.* Hogarth, London

Frankl V (1987) *Man's Search for Meaning.* Montana

Freud S (1917) *The Theory of Psychoanalysis.* Pelican Books, London

Murray-Parkes CM (1986) *Bereavement: Studies of grief in adult life.* Penguin Books, London

Stroebe M (1993) *Coping with Bereavement: a review of Grief.* Omega 26

Powers LE, Wampold BE (1999) Cognitive — behavioural factors in adjustment to adult bereavement. *Death Studies* **18**(1)

Wright B (1989) Nurses' reactions and relatives' opinions. *Bereavement Care* **81**

11

Funerals and moving forward

What are funerals for? Virtually every society throughout the world and throughout history seems to have felt a need to conduct some sort of funeral ritual, yet there remains considerable speculation about their significance. Since the funeral may be the last contact the professional palliative carer may have with the deceased, being aware of the significance of the funeral, both for the deceased and for his or her family, needs careful thought. For the informal palliative carer(s), who are often the bereaved, the funeral will have a very special poignancy.

> Try to list what you think funerals are for and why funeral rituals seem to have existed throughout history.

It might be more pertinent to ask who are funerals for? In some senses they cannot be said to be for the deceased, who are not 'present' unless we believe that they are present in spirit, and if we do believe this it seems unlikely that the spirit would be confined to the body that remains. If funerals are for the living, it is worth thinking carefully about how they can help the bereaved and what the significance is for them. Increasingly, people are being encouraged to plan their own funerals and for many this may be a meaningful activity, although it can create conflict. Look at the following instructions for a funeral and try to imagine how the bereaved might feel about carrying out the instructions:

> *No one should wear sombre clothes, and there should only be really cheerful music – I'd like something jolly, none of those sad old hymns, definitely **not** 'The Lord Is My Shepherd'!*
>
> *Let's have some readings that will make people laugh and if anyone's going to talk about me, I hope there'll be plenty of jokes. Above all, no one is to cry.*

This kind of planning is probably intended as a help to the living, but a bereaved spouse or elderly parent (or, indeed, any person who is mourning) might find it difficult to obey the instructions, and experience intense guilt because they had not done so. Sometimes the dying person will ask that a close relative or friend performs some part of the funeral ritual — gives a reading of a poem or says a prayer, maybe — which can create considerable anxiety. The bereaved person may want to comply with the wishes, but be anxious about their 'performance', concerned that they might break down at a crucial moment. (Murray-Parkes has written of his concern about this practice, which seems to be increasing, in *Bereavement Care* – the journal of CRUSE – the national bereavement charity.) The effects on the bereaved need, perhaps, to be researched.

> Try to imagine your own feelings if requested to take an active role in a funeral. Or, if you have done so, reflect on the range of feelings this aroused in you.

You may have noticed that we have used the words 'performance' and 'role'. Where else might we use these terms? As part of a discussion about a play or film the importance of the director is stressed, and it is interesting that the term 'funeral **director**' is now used more than undertaker, and plays and films need a 'director'. The funeral can be viewed as a drama in which specific acts and actions are played out and people wear recognisable 'dress', although the tradition is weakening in the UK. This perspective does not trivialise the significance of the funeral, rather the opposite, since great drama, especially great tragedy, has always had a religious or ritualistic significance.

Ritual itself can be a great support in grief. As the West has become more secular we have, to some extent, lost the language of ritual, yet there still seems to be a need to mark death in some sort of meaningful way.

> Jot down why you think the practice of leaving flowers at the scene of a death, a relatively modern phenomenon in the UK, has grown up. Sometimes the deceased were not known to those leaving tokens.

A child at a village school, which stands alongside the village church, asked me, 'Why do all these people come when somebody's died, but they don't come on Sundays?' Perhaps his rather naïve question sums up this need for ritual.

Children's presence at funerals is a much discussed issue. We have briefly looked at the pressures faced by children when a sibling receives palliative care, especially if this is prolonged. The arguments for and against the presence of children seem to range from a concern that the child might behave in a way which is somehow 'inappropriate', to a desire to protect the child from what is likely to be a powerfully emotional experience.

> Try to research whether this dilemma about children is common across cultures. It is relatively new in the UK.

For the child there may be a strong sense of exclusion if they are not allowed to be present and of considerable confusion if they are. It is surely strange that children will often bury a dead butterfly in a match box and conduct some kind of 'funeral' for it; or are helped sensitively when a pet dies, yet are anxious and confused about the funeral of, say, a loved grandparent.

> Try to recall the first funeral you were involved with and what your queries were, and whether anyone answered them.

There is a great opportunity here for using counselling skills. The child or young person needs information (an important aspect of support) and this may best be given by someone who is not a close mourner. Careful exploration of existing knowledge (or fantasies), will help to gauge the amount of information needed, and good active listening will enable checking how much depth of understanding is needed. To be effective in our use of skills, however, we need to have clarified for ourselves what our own views and feelings about funerals and their significance are.

Because funerals are common across history and cultures, some sense of ways in which their similarity may be viewed have been studied. The best known of these is that the funeral ritual represents three stages:

- separation
- transition
- integration.

Separation

The funeral is a sort of public acknowledgment that the dead are dead. It states that those that are left belong in the land of the living, and that wherever the living believe the dead now are, they are not part of this life.

> Look back at the models of grieving processes which we studied earlier. Would you see this 'separation' phase as helping to accept the reality of the death?

Transition

The time between the death and the funeral (which can vary enormously from culture to culture, and even within cultures) is a time of preparation. The living are preparing for separation. This may be a busy time, perhaps of gathering relatives, organising services, attending to practical and financial matters. The funeral marks the movement from the life that was to the life that will now have to be. It is a sort of watershed, where the bereaved see that the past is past and at the same time view the future, which may seem bleak. This may be why the funeral is sometimes seen as a **rite of passage**. Just as we mark other major life-transitions (a significant birthday, especially from adolescence to adulthood; a marriage; the birth of a baby marking parenthood), the funeral marks the transition from one status to another.

> Remind yourself of the characteristics of a transition and consider whether they could be applied to a funeral.

Integration

After a funeral, it is customary to have some kind of social gathering. It is at this gathering that the bereaved are taken into their social world integrated in their new status as widow/widower, orphan, etc. In the UK there has recently been a decline in the practice of the social gathering after a funeral, pressures of work or the more hectic pace of life mean that people 'pay their respects' at the funeral itself, but then move back to their own lives. Interestingly, in past centuries, the gathering was a more elaborate (and expensive) affair than the funeral itself. Perhaps the amount of money spent (often on funeral gifts for the guests) was intended as an indicator of the dead person's status. (Certainly the type of coffin used can vary hugely in cost: another indicator of where the emphasis now lies maybe?)

> In your view is the decline in the social occasion therapeutic to those who grieve or not?

Opinions seem to vary as to the benefit of the social gathering; some bereaved people find them a terrible ordeal while others appreciate the support. The help given to the bereaved by the social gathering can be a reassurance that they are wanted and valued in their new status. The following table shows the results of a survey into the help given around the time of the funeral.

Ways in which family and friends helped the bereaved after the death				
		Status of bereaved		
	Total	Widow	Widower	Other
	758	312	125	321
Kinds of help specified	%	%	%	%
Helping to arrange the funeral, eg. seeing the undertaker, contacting relatives, providing refreshments	57	57	58	56
Accompanying the bereaved when contacting officials or making funeral arrangements	35	32	41	35
Contacting 'officials', eg. seeing the registrar or coroner, notifying insurance company or employer of deceased, sorting out deceased's affairs	33	43	25	27
Providing comfort or moral support, eg. staying with the bereaved, looking after the bereaved or his/her children	15	19	21	8
Sorting through and disposing of deceased's possessions	4	0	8	6
Giving advice to the bereaved	3	3	2	9

Do you find it interesting that most of the help was practical? Counselling skills can be useful in practical support, but perhaps even more helpful in the less active support of 'being' rather than 'doing'. Although some people find funerals an ordeal and others see them as anything from a celebration of a life to a simple requirement to dispose decently of the body, their universal nature indicates that they fulfil some kind of human need. If we are to use counselling skills therapeutically at such a significant time we need to be clear what their personal meaning is for us, especially as funerals confront us with the fact of our own mortality — at some future time, others will attend our funeral.

Since the funeral often marks the end of palliative care and a time of moving forward this may be an opportune time to review counselling skills and to consider a framework or model which may help us to structure our use of them. The best known model of counselling or helping skills is that of Gerard Egan (1999) who suggests that helping can be structured as:

- explore
- understand
- act.

with skills appropriate to each phase of both a helping interview and a helping relationship. Very simplistically this could be seen as:

- helping the other person (whether dying patient, bereaved relative/carer or colleague) to explore their difficulties or problems **from their own perspective**. It is important to keep remembering that we are not doing the exploring, but are using the skills to facilitate another's exploration of their concerns
- enabling the person to gain a new perspective on or understanding of their situation (perhaps by seeing how they might be contributing to it) and to begin considering how they might begin to change things or move forward
- facilitating some movement towards change, by helping with goals and strategies which best fit their resources and circumstances.

Sometimes these three phases are described as:

- ❖ The current scenario   (the state of things which needs help)
- ❖ The preferred scenario   (what things would look like if they were [a bit] better)

❖ Getting there   (how to move towards a way of
                                   living that is more satisfying)

> Review some helping interviews or relationships in which you have
> been involved — either as giver or receiver — and consider whether
> they have, broadly speaking, followed this process.

Human beings are fortunately (or maybe unfortunately) so complex that
a straight path through each stage is rarely likely and perhaps not even
possible. Another way of looking at the model might be:

Egan's three-stage model of helping

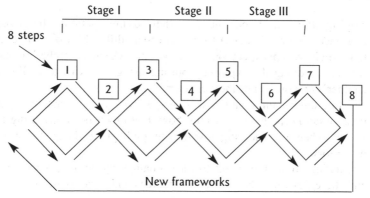

Evaluating may throw up more areas to work through

National Extension College, Counselling Skills

Step 1   Explore, opens out areas
Step 2   Focus, narrows down
Step 3   New perspectives or frameworks, open up understanding
Step 4   Goal setting, focuses down
Step 5   Exploring and generating methods, opens up creativity
Step 6   Evaluating and choosing a method or methods, narrows down
Step 7   Planning to implement, opens up
Step 8   Evaluating, brings together

A further way of viewing the model (or 'map' as it is sometimes called)
is to see it more as a circle where it is possible for the process to move
back and fore as new issues or insights arise. This avoids any concern that

following a linear path might be too rigid or could prevent us listening to the full range of emotions which might be shared with us, because we are over-influenced by the three phases as progress.

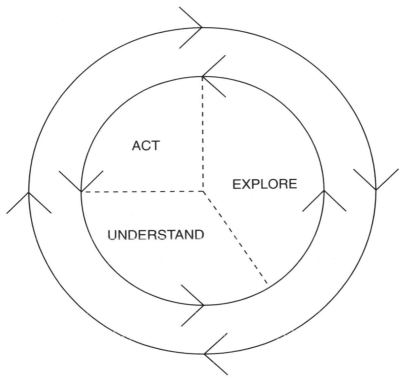

The divisions between each stage or phase are represented as broken lines, to indicate that the amount of time or work spent on each may vary. The arrows indicate that the process may swing from one phase to another, rather than move along a path.

> Review your own practice and reflect on whether it follows (more or less) a similar structure.

A sensitive user of skills will be alert to where a patient or client might be in the process and be careful to work at their pace, rather then be governed by the structure of the model.

Within any version of the model, it will be evident that some skills are more likely to belong in one phase than in another. It would, for instance, be inappropriate or even impossible to plan for action, however limited, before helping the other person to explore their thoughts and feelings about their problem area. Or rather, if we did, we would be imposing what we think is best for the client/patient.

> Using the circle diagram, or perhaps drawing one of your own, try to 'allocate' the skills we earlier identified to each phase.

(At the end of this chapter you will find a suggested way of 'allocating' skills, but you may also find it useful to look at the latest version of Egan's model (1999) which has some variations).

Throughout this book it has been emphasised that counselling skills would be no more than mechanical techniques if they are not imbued with qualities. The way we are with people is often much more important than what we do with (or for) them. A further way of looking at a model for using counselling skills in palliative care is to see the structure of the helping interview, or the structure of the whole helping relationship, in terms of 'being' as well as in terms of 'doing'. The following model may provide the way forward and provide you with a framework which is therapeutic for the people for whom you provide care, and helpful for you in terms of moving forward in your valuable work.

	Setting off	Middle ground	Endings
What is going on	**'Coming together'**	**Working together**	**'Letting go'**
(Process)	• Establishing boundaries • Negotiating contracts • Establishing relation-ships • Assessing • Acknowledging fears and anxieties • Acceptance of reluc-tance to engage	• Widening explored issues • Exploring feelings • Deepening the relationship • Enabling insight and understanding • Holding boundaries • Offering links and connections • Identifying themes • Maybe re-working	• Looking at self ~ others ~ life context ~ illness • Separation • Loss (for all parties)
Being (qualities)	• Empathy • Acceptance • Genuineness • Trust • Being 'open' • Balancing hope and realism	• All qualities from setting off, plus • More advanced empathy • Sharing self • Listening to self • Checking patient/client's use of self	• All qualities from setting off and middle ground, plus • Acknowledging work done • Equality of regard
Doing (skills)	• Active listening • Observing • Accurate responding • Paraphrase • Reflection • Summary • Giving information • Acknowledge difficulties • Identifying strengths	• Everything from beginning plus • Sensing • Focusing/being concrete • Using immediacy • Negotiating goals	• All skills from beginnings and middle ground, plus • Reviewing work done • Possibly referring • Saying goodbye

As a final review of your understanding of this and previous chapters, reflect on the following questions and try to formulate answers which are valid for your personal practice.

1. How helpful to palliative care is it to develop some theoretical understanding of loss? In a discussion about working with loss and grief, Worden said, 'Any counselling or therapy should be based on a solid theoretical understanding of human personality and behaviours and not be merely a set of techniques' (1983). **How far** would you agree with his view about the need for theoretical understanding? **To what extent** does theory underpin or help your palliative care?

2. *There's night and day, brother, both sweet things;*
   Sun moon and stars, brother, all sweet things;
   There's likewise a wind on the heath..
   Life is very sweet, brother;
   Who would wish to die?   (George Borrow, Lavengro)
   Distinguishing wishes from needs is a difficult task for palliative carers. Reflect on your view of patient values, especially if the patient does wish to die and seeks help to do so. How realistic do you find it to keep hope alive, while being aware that false hope would not be congruent with the core quality of sincerity or genuiness and that not being genuine can, in turn, lead to distancing?

3. How feasible is holistic communication (both from the transmitter's and the receiver's perspectives)? What are the likely barriers? Reflect on the degree to which self-awareness can help us overcome our personal barriers.

4. The British Association for Counselling and Psychotherapy are very firm about the difference between counselling and using counselling skills to enhance a functional role. How helpful or challenging do you find this distinction? What responsibilities does it place on the user of counselling skills (eg. in terms of boundaries)?

5. What is the difference between a theory and a model? Which aspects of a model help you to plan emotional support for dying people and their relatives? Can a model help you in closing contact?

References

Egan G (1999) *The Skilled Helper.* Brooks-Cole Publishing Company, California

Hennessy PJ (1980) *Families, Funerals and Finances.* Research Report No 6. HMSO, London

Van Gennep A (1977) *The Rites of Passage.* Routledge, London

Worden JW (1983) *Grief Counselling and Grief Therapy.* Tavistock, London

Index

Q

quality of life   41

R

reflection   79
respect   62, 79, 95
rights
   ~ of people with cancer   17
Rogers, Carl   47

S

sedation   112
self-awareness   29, 30, 55, 56, 66, 101
self-disclosure   87
'shoulds' and 'oughts'   95
silence   79
   ~ responding to   80
silence threshold   79
sincerity   47, 54, 55, 62, 66
sleep disturbance   168
social withdrawal   37
spiritual pain   173, 174
spirituality   172

suspected awareness   53

T

theory of attachment   5
time-line   32, 57
transition   7
   ~ model of   7
trust   55

U

unconditional positive regard   69
use of touch   80

V

values   62

W

Walter, Tony   46
wants, of a dying person   20
Weisman   40
why? questions   77
World Health Organization (WHO)   18